LABORATORY EQUIPMENT

Label the following pieces of laboratory equipment.

Name _____

a. Bunsen burner
b. balance
c. funnel

d. tongs
e. ring stand
f. Erlenmeyer flask

h. graduated cylinder
i. test tube
j. test tube clamp

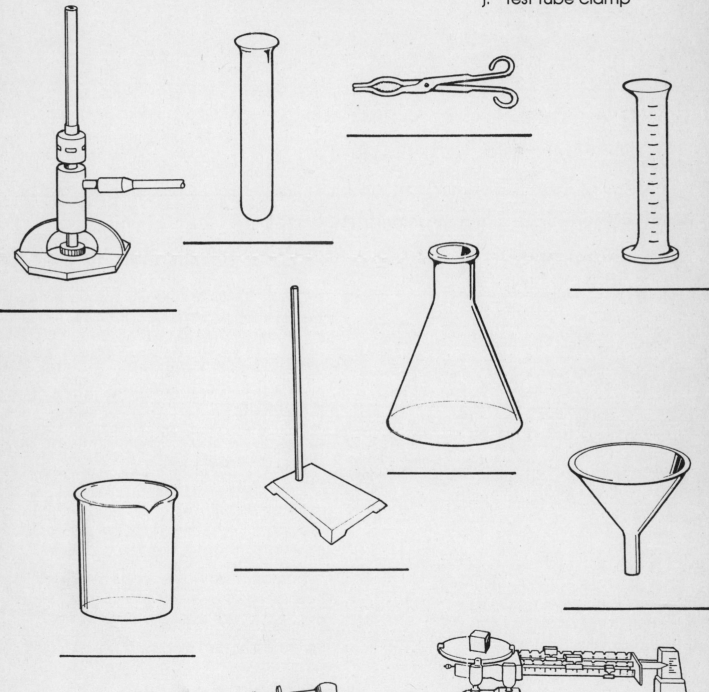

THE SCIENTIFIC METHOD

Name _____

Put the following steps of the scientific method in the proper order.

_____ Organize and analyze data

_____ State a hypothesis

_____ Identify the problem

_____ State conclusion

_____ Design and carry out an experiment

_____ Make observations and record data

_____ Gather information

Match the term in Column I with its definition in Column II.

Column I

1. theory _____

2. law _____

3. hypothesis _____

4. experiment _____

5. variable _____

6. control _____

7. data _____

8. conclusion _____

9. application _____

Column II

a. suggested explanation to a problem or observation based upon known information

b. used to test a hypothesis

c. anything that can affect the results of an experiment

d. observations and measurements made during an experiment

e. part within the experiment that is maintained without change in order to provide a comparison for the part of the experiment containing the variable

f. hypothesis that has been tested and supported by a great amount of evidence over a long period of time

g. statement describing (but not explaining) a natural event or phenomenon

h. new use to which results are put or new technique developed

i. a summary that explains whether or not the data support the hypothesis

THE SYSTEME INTERNATIONAL D'UNITES (SI)

Name _____

The measuring system used in science is the SI, which was adopted according to an international agreement reached in 1960. It is based on the metric system. The standard units in SI are:

Property	Unit	Symbol
mass	kilogram	kg
distance	meter	m
time	second	s
electric current	Ampere	A
temperature	Kelvin	K
amount of substance	mole	mol

As with the metric system, the SI utilizes prefixes to change the value of units. The following units are frequently used in science:

Prefix	Symbol	Value
mega-	M	1 000 000
kilo-	k	1 000
deci-	d	0.1
centi-	c	0.01
milli-	m	0.001
micro-	μ	0.000 001
nano-	n	0.000 000 0001

Example:
How many meters are equivalent to 500 mm?

$$500 \text{ mm} \times \frac{1 \text{ m}}{1\,000 \text{ mm}} = 0.5 \text{ m}$$

Make the following conversions within the SI.

1. 3.0 m = _____ cm

2. 1,500 mL = _____ L

3. 35 cg = _____ g

4. 0.05 m = _____ mm

5. 2.5 L = _____ mL

6. 0.25 km = _____ m

7. 50,000 μm = _____ m

8. 0.015 g = _____ mg

9. 75 cL = _____ L

10. 2,750 mg = _____ g

What would be a reasonable unit to use to measure the following?

11. distance from earth to moon _____

12. length of a bacterium _____

13. mass of a bowling ball _____

14. mass of an aspirin tablet _____

15. dropperful of medicine _____

3

SELF QUIZ—SCIENTIFIC METHOD AND THE SI SYSTEM

Name _____

Circle the letter of the correct answer.

1. In an experiment, one ____ is tested at a time to determine how it affects results.

    a. control   b. variable   c. problem   d. observation

2. The ____ describes the use of equipment and materials in an experiment.

    a. procedure   b. conclusion   c. control   d. problem

3. A ____ is the part of an experiment that provides a reliable standard for comparison.

    a. procedure   b. theory   c. variable   d. control

4. The information already recorded about a scientific subject is the scientific ____ .

    a. record   b. method   c. technique   d. experiment

5. ____ are the recorded facts and measurements from an experiment.

    a. Procedures   b. Data   c. Theories   d. Inferences

6. The practical use of scientific knowledge is called ____ .

    a. research   b. inferring   c. procedure   d. technology

7. A ____ is an explanation of observations that have been tested many times.

    a. conclusion   b. hypothesis   c. theory   d. record

8. A(n) ____ is a suggested solution to a scientific problem.

    a. observation   b. hypothesis   c. problem   d. procedure

9. Instruments and our senses are used to make ____ during an experiment.

    a. observations   b. hypotheses   c. problems   d. controls

10. A(n) ____ is performed under carefully controlled conditions to test a hypothesis.

    a. activity   b. observation   c. inference   d. experiment

11. A scientific ____ describes how nature works.

    a. record   b. law   c. hypothesis   d. result

12. To be accepted, a scientific discovery must produce ____ each time it is tested.

    a. the same results   b. the same hypothesis   c. new conclusions   d. new data

13. If after numerous tests a major hypothesis cannot be shown to be false, it may be accepted as ____ .

    a. a control   b. a theory   c. data   d. an observation

14. New observations that do not agree with an accepted theory may cause the theory to be ____ .

    a. explained   b. rejected   c. proven   d. recognized

15. A ____ is a logical explanation to a problem based on observation.

     a. control   b. theory   c. conclusion d. procedure

16. The commonly used unit in the measurement of temperature in the Biology laboratory is the ____ .

     a. Kelvin   b. Celsius   c. Fahrenheit d. boiling point

17. The ____ is the unit of time in the SI system.

     a. day   b. second   c. minute   d. hour

18. A ____ is a fixed quantity used for comparison.

     a. procedure   b. variable   c. standard   d. prefix

19. The unit of mass commonly used in the laboratory is the ____ .

     a. meter   b. cubic meter   c. gram   d. kilometer

20. The space occupied by an object is its ____ .

     a. volume   b. height   c. width   d. length

21. The amount of matter in an object is its ____ .

     a. mass   b. volume   c. size   d. balance

22. A scale commonly used by scientists for measuring temperature is the ____ scale.

     a. degree   b. Celsius c. boiling point   d. Fahrenheit

23. There are ____ in one kilogram.

     a. 0.001 grams   b. 1000 milligrams   c. 0.001 milligrams   d. 1000 grams

24. Standards are important for comparing observations and are used ____ .

     a. by everyone   c. only for counting things

     b. only in tropical rainforests   d. only in scientific experiments

25. One-hundredth of a meter is written as a ____ .

     a. decimeter   b. millimeter   c. centimeter   d. kilometer

26. How many millimeters make a centimeter?

     a. 100   b. 10   c. 1000   d. 0.10

27. A prefix meaning one thousand standard units is ____ .

     a. milli-   b. centi-   c. kilo-   d. deci-

28. On the Celsius scale, water boils at what temperature?

     a. 32 degrees   b. 212 degrees   c. 0 degrees   d. 100 degrees

29. 50 cc of water would equal which quantity?

     a. 5000 mL   b. 500 mL   c. 50 mL   d. 0.5 L

30. Which of the following units would we use to measure the distance to Australia?

     a. millimeters   b. centimeters   c. kilometers   d. kilograms

THE COMPOUND MICROSCOPE

Name _____

Label each of the following parts on the diagram of a compound microscope. Describe the purpose/use of each part.

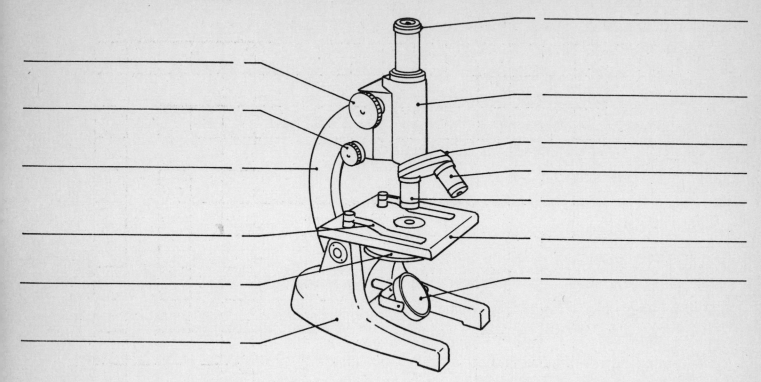

1. base _____

2. mirror _____

3. stage _____

4. arm _____

5. fine adjustment _____

6. coarse adjustment _____

7. eyepiece _____

8. body tube _____

9. nosepiece _____

10. high power objective _____

11. low power objective _____

12. clip _____

13. diaphragm _____

MICROSCOPE CROSSWORD

Name _____

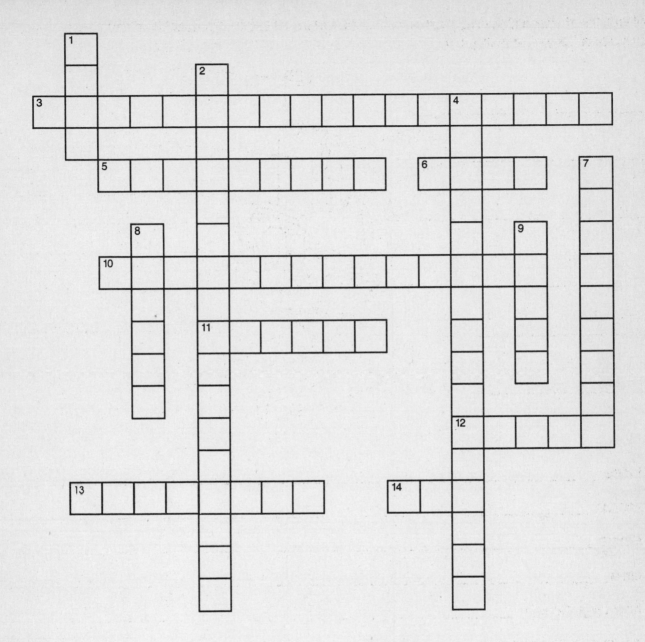

Across

3. Lens that allows greater magnification
5. Regulates the amount of light
6. The microscope rests on this.
10. Used for final focusing
11. Eyepiece
12. Platform upon which to mount the slide
13. Holds eyepiece lens at top and objective lens at bottom
14. Holds the tube and stage, and attaches them to the base

Down

1. Holds the slide in place
2. Lens used to locate the specimen
4. Used for first focusing
7. Rotating piece that holds objective lens
8. Reflects light to the specimen
9. Chemical sometimes used to make the specimen visible

STATES OF MATTER

Name _____

Complete the following table by placing a check mark in each of the first three columns as it applies. Then, identify its state as solid, liquid or gas in the last column.

Example	Definite Shape	Definite Volume	Takes Shape of Container	State of Matter
1. water at 25°C				
2. ice at -4°C				
3. steam at 105°C				
4. iron				
5. air				
6. carbon dioxide at 20°C				
7. juice				
8. wood				
9. oil				
10. nitrogen at room temperature				
11. milk				
12. ozone				
13. glass				
14. coffee				
15. chalk				

CHEMICAL vs. PHYSICAL CHANGE

Name _____

In a physical change, the original substance still exists, it has only changed in form. Energy changes usually do not accompany physical changes, except in phase changes and when substances dissolve.

In a chemical change, a new substance is produced. Energy changes always accompany chemical changes. Physical changes usually accompany chemical changes.

Classify the following as being either a chemical or a physical change.

1. Sodium chloride dissolves in water. _____

2. Hydrochloric acid reacts with sodium hydroxide to produce a salt, water and heat. _____

3. A pellet of sodium is sliced in half. _____

4. Water is heated and changed to steam. _____

5. Food is digested. _____

6. Starch molecules are formed from smaller glucose molecules. _____

7. Ice melts. _____

8. Plant leaves lose water through evaporation. _____

9. A red blood cell placed in distilled water will swell and burst. _____

10. The energy in food molecules is transferred into molecules of ATP. _____

11. The roots of a plant absorb water. _____

12. Iron rusts. _____

13. Oxygen is incorporated into hemoglobin to bring it to the cells. _____

14. A person gets cooler by perspiring. _____

15. Proteins are made from amino acids. _____

16. A match burns. _____

17. A toothpick is broken in half. _____

ELEMENTS, COMPOUNDS AND MIXTURES

Name _____

An element consists of only one kind of atom. A compound consists of two or more different elements chemically combined in a fixed ratio. The components of a mixture can be in any proportion and are not chemically bound.

Classify each of the following as an element, compound or mixture by writing E, C or M in the space provided.

1. sodium _____

2. water _____

3. soil _____

4. coffee _____

5. oxygen _____

6. alcohol _____

7. carbon dioxide _____

8. cake batter _____

9. air _____

10. soap _____

11. iron _____

12. salt water _____

13. ice cream _____

14. nitrogen _____

15. eggs _____

16. blood _____

17. table salt _____

18. nail polish _____

19. milk _____

20. cola _____

21. orange juice _____

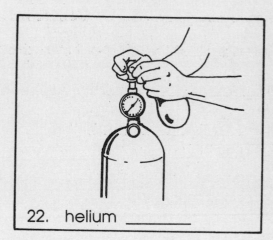

22. helium _____

23. methane _____

ELEMENT SYMBOLS

Name _____

Write the symbol for the following elements which are common in living things.

1. oxygen _____

2. hydrogen _____

3. chlorine _____

4. potassium _____

5. fluorine _____

6. manganese _____

7. carbon _____

8. zinc _____

9. sodium _____

10. sulfur _____

11. phosphorus _____

12. iodine _____

13. magnesium _____

14. nitrogen _____

15. copper _____

16. iron _____

17. calcium _____

18. cobalt _____

Write the name of the element indicated by each of the following symbols.

19. As _____

20. Pb _____

21. Kr _____

22. Ba _____

23. He _____

24. Ne _____

25. Si _____

26. U _____

27. Sn _____

28. Pt _____

29. Rn _____

30. Al _____

31. Cu _____

32. Ag _____

33. Pu _____

34. Sr _____

35. Am _____

36. Au _____

37. Ra _____

38. Ge _____

39. Br _____

40. Hg _____

PARTS OF THE ATOM

Name _____

Using the Periodic Table of the Elements, determine the number of protons, neutrons and electrons in each of the following atoms. Draw a model of the atom showing the electrons in the proper energy levels.

1. $^{1}_{1}H$ ____ protons
                  ____ neutrons
                  ____ electrons

2. $^{12}_{6}C$ ____ protons
                   ____ neutrons
                   ____ electrons

3. $^{23}_{11}Na$ ____ protons
                     ____ neutrons
                     ____ electrons

4. $^{31}_{15}P$ ____ protons
                    ____ neutrons
                    ____ electrons

5. $^{16}_{8}O$ ____ protons
                   ____ neutrons
                   ____ electrons

IONIC vs. COVALENT BONDS

Name _____

When nonmetals chemically bond they do so by sharing electrons. The bond is called a covalent bond. When an active metal and a nonmetal bond, the active metal transfers one or more electrons to the nonmetal. This bond is called an ionic bond. Ionic compounds (except for bases) are also called salts.

Classify the following compounds as ionic or covalent.

1. $CaCl_2$ _____

2. CO_2 _____

3. H_2O _____

4. $BaCl_2$ _____

5. O_2 _____

6. NaF _____

7. NaS _____

8. S_8 _____

9. SO_3 _____

10. LiBr _____

11. MgO _____

12. C_2H_5OH _____

13. HCl _____

14. N_2 _____

15. NaI _____

16. NO_2 _____

17. Al_2O_3 _____

18. $FeCl_3$ _____

19. P_2O_5 _____

20. N_2O_3 _____

21. H_2 _____

22. K_2O _____

23. KI _____

24. P_4 _____

25. CH_4 _____

26. NaCl _____

Draw an electron shell diagram of the ionic compound calcium oxide, CaO.

Draw an electron shell diagram of the covalent compound methane, CH_4.

BALANCING EQUATIONS

Name _____

Balance the following chemical equations.

1. $Na + I_2 \rightarrow NaI$

2. $N_2 + O_2 \rightarrow N_2O$

3. $N_2 + H_2 \rightarrow NH_3$

4. $CH_4 + O_2 \rightarrow CO_2 + H_2O$

5. $KI + Cl_2 \rightarrow KCl + I_2$

6. $S + O_2 \rightarrow SO_3$

7. $H_2O_2 \rightarrow H_2O + O_2$

8. $Na + H_2O \rightarrow NaOH + H_2$

9. $H_2O \rightarrow H_2 + O_2$

10. $KClO_3 \rightarrow KCl + O_2$

11. $K_3PO_4 + HCl \rightarrow KCl + H_3PO_4$

12. $CO_2 + H_2O \rightarrow H_2CO_3$

13. $K_2O + H_2O \rightarrow KOH$

14. $Mg + HCl \rightarrow MgCl_2 + H_2$

15. $KOH + H_2SO_4 \rightarrow K_2SO_4 + H_2O$

SELF QUIZ—ATOMIC STRUCTURE AND EQUATIONS

Name _____

Circle the letter of the correct answer.

1. A(n) ____ is a substance made up of one kind of atom.
    a. compound   b. element   c. mixture   d. enzyme

2. The smallest particle of an element having the properties of that element is a(n) ____ .
    a. atom   b. compound   c. molecule   d. enzyme

3. A(n) ____ is matter made of substances that are not chemically bonded together.
    a. mixture   b. element   c. compound   d. molecule

4. The correctly written symbol for chlorine is ____ .
    a. C   b. CL   c. Ch   d. Cl

5. How many atoms of hydrogen are in each molecule of table sugar, $C_{12}H_{22}O_{11}$?
    a. 11   b. 12   c. 22   d. 45

6. Which of the following is a compound?
    a. iron   b. blood   c. carbon dioxide   d. air

7. A(n) ____ contains two or more atoms bonded together.
    a. mixture   b. molecule   c. atom   d. element

8. A substance that contains two or more different kinds of atoms bonded together is ____ .
    a. an element   b. oxygen   c. energy   d. a compound

9. How many atoms of oxygen are represented in the equation: $C + O_2 \rightarrow CO_2$?
    a. 1   b. 2   c. 3   d. 4

10. The smallest part of a compound that still has the properties of that compound is a(n) ____ .
    a. atom   b. cell   c. molecule   d. element

11. An atom that contains 15 protons and 10 neutrons within its nucleus will have an atomic mass of ____ amu.
    a. 5   b. 10   c. 15   d. 25

12. An atom of atomic number 12 and mass number 22 contains how many protons?
    a. 10   b. 12   c. 22   d. 34

13. The atom described in Problem 12 will have how many electrons?
    a. 10   b. 12   c. 22   d. 34

14. The atom described in Problem 12 will have how many neutrons?
    a. 10   b. 12   c. 22   d. 34

15. Elements combine by losing, sharing or gaining ____ .
    a. electrons   b. protons   c. neutrons   d. molecules

ACID, BASE OR SALT?

Name _____

Classify each of the following as an acid, a base or a salt.

1. HNO_3 _____

2. $NaOH$ _____

3. $NaNO_3$ _____

4. HCl _____

5. KCl _____

6. $Ba(OH)_2$ _____

7. KOH _____

8. H_2S _____

9. $Al(NO_2)_3$ _____

10. H_2SO_4 _____

11. $CaCl_2$ _____

12. H_3PO_4 _____

13. Na_2SO_4 _____

14. $Mg(OH)_2$ _____

15. H_2CO_3 _____

16. NH_4OH _____

17. NH_4Cl _____

18. HBr _____

19. $FeBr_3$ _____

20. HF _____

21. $NaCl$ _____

22. $Ca(OH)_2$ _____

23. $HC_2H_3O_2$ _____

24. $CuCl_2$ _____

25. HNO_2 _____

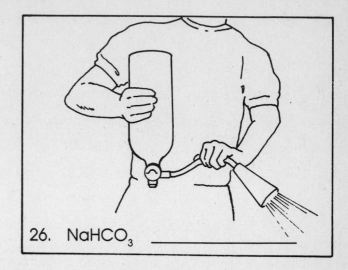

26. $NaHCO_3$ _____

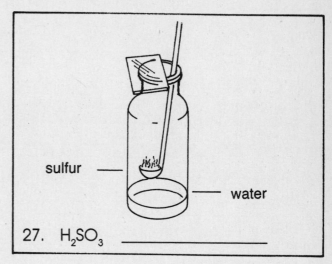

sulfur

water

27. H_2SO_3 _____

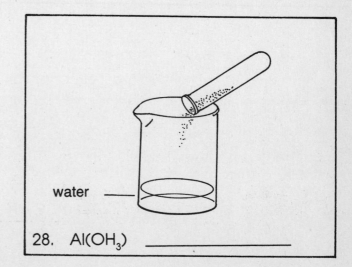

water

28. $Al(OH_3)$ _____

pH

pH is a scale that measures the hydronium ion concentration of a solution. A pH of less than 7 indicates an acidic solution. A solution with a pH of 7 is neutral. A solution with a pH of 7 to 14 is basic and contains a higher concentration of hydroxide ions than hydronium ions.

Indicators are substances that change color in the presence of certain irons. Phenolphthalein is colorless in an acid and a neutral solution, pink in a base. Litmus is red in an acid, blue in a base.

For each of the following substances indicate the pH range expected: acid = pH < 7, neutral = pH = 7, or base = pH > 7 indicate the color the indicator will appear, and state the solution's use.

Solution	pH Range	Phenol-phtalein	Blue Litmus	Red Litmus	Use
vinegar					
soap					
cola					
ammonia					
rain					
Milk of Magnesia					
milk					
saliva					
coffee					
gastric juices					
human blood					
orange juice					
Kool-Aid					
drain cleaner					
bleach					
shampoo					

INORGANIC vs. ORGANIC COMPOUNDS

Name _____

Matter is often classified as organic or inorganic. Indicate the class for each type of matter. Then, identify its major properties as that of a salt, acid, base, protein, lipid, nucleic acid or carbohydrate.

Matter	Class	Properties of
1. HCl	_____	_____
2. DNA	_____	_____
3. starch	_____	_____
4. KOH	_____	_____
5. sodium chloride	_____	_____
6. skin	_____	_____
7. animal fat	_____	_____
8. glucose	_____	_____
9. vegetable oil	_____	_____
10. hair	_____	_____
11. RNA	_____	_____
12. sucrose	_____	_____
13. butter	_____	_____
14. fingernails	_____	_____
15. H_2SO_4	_____	_____
16. HNO_3	_____	_____
17. gelatin	_____	_____
18. molasses	_____	_____
19. vinegar	_____	_____

DEHYDRATION SYNTHESIS

Name _____

In the following two examples of dehydration synthesis, show how the removal of the water molecule(s) takes place by drawing a ring around the components of water. Then, draw the structural formula of each product.

Synthesis of a Fat

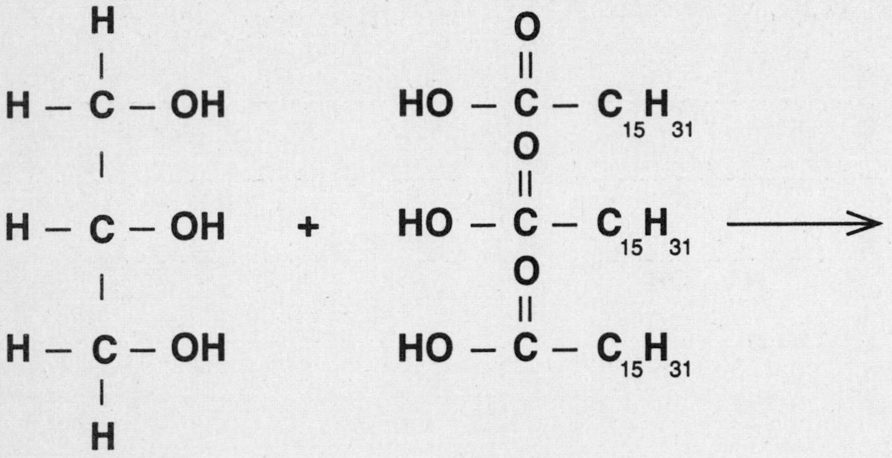

```
        H                          O
        |                          ||
   H — C — OH          HO — C — C  H
        |                          15 31
        |                          O
        |                          ||
   H — C — OH    +     HO — C — C  H      ⟶
        |                          15  31
        |                          O
        |                          ||
   H — C — OH          HO — C — C  H
        |                          15 31
        H
```

| 1 glycerol molecule | + | 3 fatty acid molecules | ⟶ | 1 fat molecule | + | 3 water molecules |

Formation of a Peptide Bond

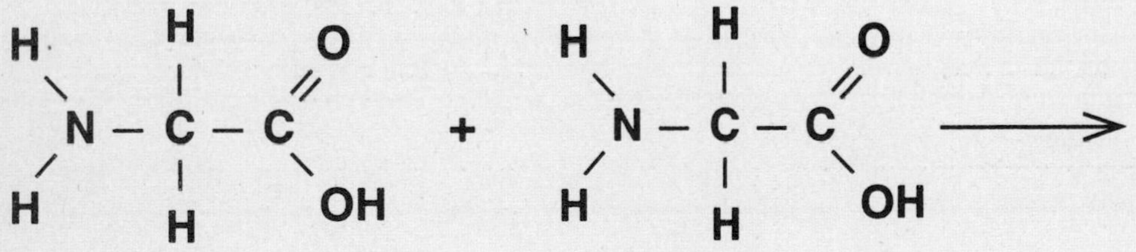

```
  H     H     O              H     H     O
   \    |     ||              \    |     ||
    N — C — C          +       N — C — C         ⟶
   /    |     \               /    |     \
  H     H      OH            H     H      OH
```

| amino acid | + | amino acid | ⟶ |

dipeptide   +   water

HYDROLYSIS

Hydrolysis is the opposite of a dehydration synthesis. A large molecule is broken down into two or more smaller molecules by the addition of water.

Draw the structural formulas of the expected products in the two following hydrolysis reactions.

Breakdown of a Disaccharide to Monosaccharides

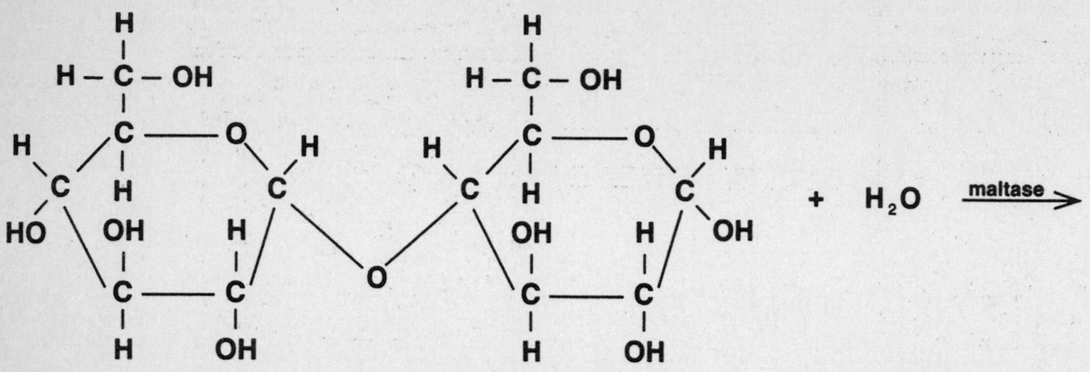

disaccharide

2 monosaccharides

Breakdown of a Lipid

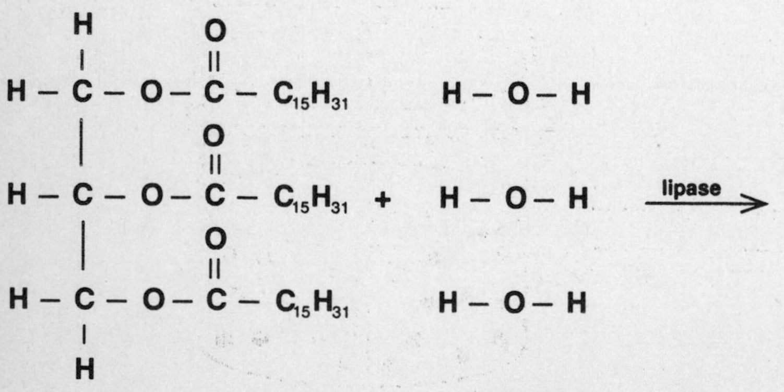

| lipid | + | 3 water molecules | lipase → | glycerol | 3 fatty acids |

20

DIFFUSIONS AND OSMOSIS

Name _____

The diagrams below show what each solution would look like after a period of time has passed. Label each as osmosis or diffusion.

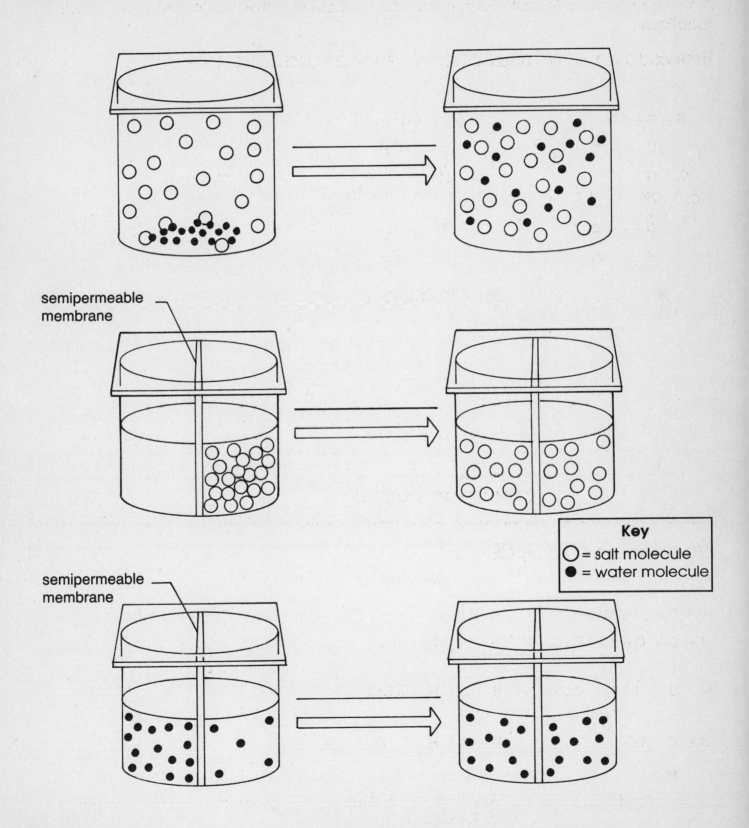

semipermeable membrane

semipermeable membrane

Key
◯ = salt molecule
● = water molecule

LIFE ACTIVITIES AND BODY SYSTEMS

Name _____

Match the life activity in Column I with its example in Column II.

Column I

1. nutrition _____
2. circulation _____
3. respiration _____
4. excretion _____
5. synthesis _____
6. regulation _____
7. growth _____
8. reproduction _____
9. metabolism _____
10. homeostasis _____
11. digestion _____

Column II

a. a cat has a litter of six kittens

b. the cells utilize glucose to produce energy

c. a plant absorbs minerals from the soil

d. a plant forms large starch molecules from smaller sugar molecules

e. the bloodstream brings oxygen and food to the cells

f. waste products are eliminated during perspiration

g. a person sweats to keep body temperature at a safe level

h. the brain coordinates the various systems of the body

i. process by which food is changed into a form the body can use

j. the human body produces hormones, vitamins, proteins, enzymes, etc. to keep it functioning

k. a 7-pound baby becomes a 180-pound man

Fill in the blanks with the correct body systems.

The lungs are the main organ of the _____ system, but they are also an

organ in the _____ system. The lymph and the lymphatics are part of the

_____ system. Although food does not pass through the liver and gall

bladder, they are part of the _____ system. As a duct gland, the pancreas

is part of the _____ system. As a ductless gland, the pancreas is part of the

_____ system. The hypothalamus, through its neurosecretory cells,

coordinates the activities of the _____ and _____ systems.

LIFE ACTIVITIES CROSSWORD

Name _____

Across

1. process of producing more organisms in order to continue the species

5. information acquired by chemical stimuli or response to the environment that is directed to the brain

6. a chemical messenger that is produced in one part of an organism and triggers a reaction in another part of the organism

7. Response of the body to invasion of foreign substances

11. The organism's actions as a result of sensory, neural, and hormonal factors in response to changes in external or internal conditions

14. The ingestion of food for energy and to provide vitamins and minerals the body cannot make for itself

15. The breakdown of foods into molecules the body can use

16. Distribution of materials within an organism

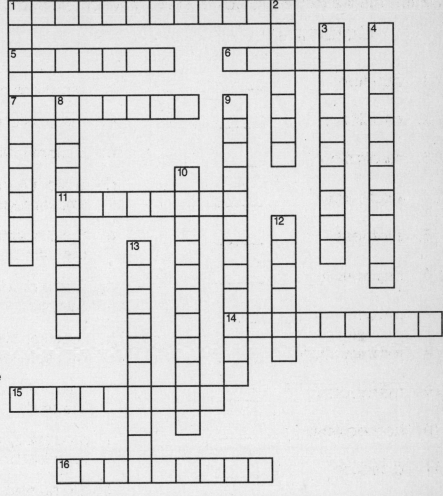

Down

1. The utilization of oxygen and release of carbon dioxide

2. System that relays commands to skeletal muscles and stimulates glands and other muscle so the organism may continue to live and respond to stimuli

3. Ability to independently move about from place to place

4. Series of changes, beginning with conception, an organism undergoes until the adult stage is reached

8. The sum of all chemical processes within a living cell or organism

9. The homeostatic state of water in an organism

10. The transport of material from one place to another within an organism through the use of internal fluid

12. An organism's increase in size or number of cells, with no developmental changes

13. Control and coordination of all the activities of an organism

AUTOTROPHS VS. HETEROTROPHS

Name _____

An autotroph is an organism that is capable of forming organic compounds from inorganic compounds in its environment. In other words, an autotroph can make its own food. Heterotrophs must get their food from other organisms.

Classify the following organisms as an autotroph (a) or a heterotroph (h).

1. maple tree _____
2. human _____
3. wheat _____
4. fungi _____
5. ameba _____
6. green algae _____
7. housefly _____
8. fern _____
9. dandelion _____
10. goldfish _____

11. grass _____
12. cow _____

Most autotrophic nutrition is a result of photosynthesis. Heterotrophic nutrition involves the taking in and processing of food and the elimination of wastes. Classify the following as related primarily to autotrophic nutrition (a) or heterotrophic nutrition (h).

13. chlorophyll _____
14. digestion _____
15. phagocytosis _____
16. photolysis _____
17. rhizoids _____
18. lipase _____
19. carbon fixation _____
20. pseudopods _____
21. PGAL _____
22. light reaction _____

23. maltose _____
24. CO_2 is used _____
25. ingestion _____
26. chloroplasts _____
27. dark reaction _____
28. grana _____
29. proteose _____
30. glucose production _____
31. stroma _____
32. bile _____

ANIMAL CELLS

Label the organelles in the diagram below of a typical animal cell. Describe the function/purpose of each organelle in the cell.

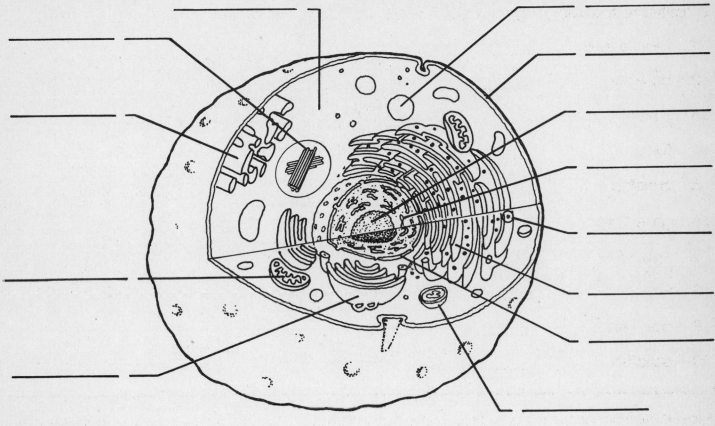

a. vacuole _____

b. lysosome_____

c. ribosomes _____

d. Golgi complex _____

e. cytoplasm _____

f. nucleus _____

g. nucleolus _____

h. nuclear membrane_____

i. cell (plasma) membrane _____

j. mitochondria _____

k. smooth endoplasmic reticulum_____

l. rough endoplasmic reticulum _____

m. centriole _____

25

PLANT CELLS

Label the organelles in the diagram below of a typical plant cell. Describe the function/purpose of each organelle in the cell.

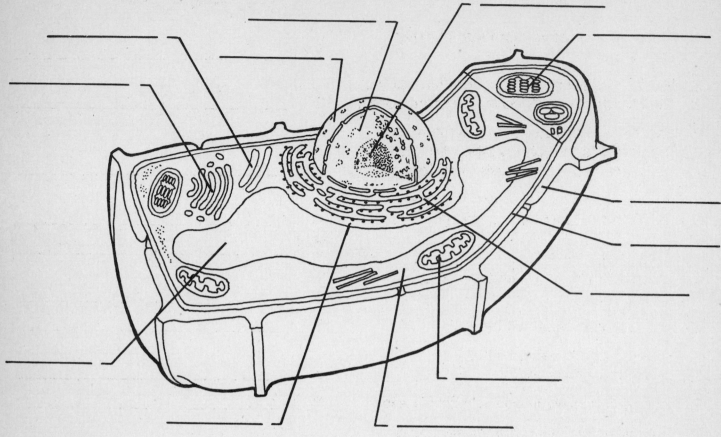

a. ribosomes _____

b. Golgi complex _____

c. cytoplasm _____

d. nucleus _____

e. nucleolus _____

f. nuclear membrane _____

g. cell (plasma) membrane _____

h. mitochondria _____

i. rough endoplasmic reticulum _____

j. vacuole _____

k. cell wall _____

l. chloroplast _____

m. smooth endoplasmic reticulum _____

FUNCTION OF THE ORGANELLES

Name _____

Which organelle performs each of the following functions within the cell?

Function

Organelle

1. Controls the movement into and out of the cell

1. _____

2. Watery material which contains many of the materials involved in cell metabolism

2. _____

3. Serves as a pathway for the transport of materials throughout the cell; also associated with synthesis and storage

3. _____

4. Serves as the control center for cell metabolism and reproduction

4. _____

5. Sites of protein synthesis

5. _____

6. Involved in the digestion of food within the cell

6. _____

7. The "powerhouse" of the cell

7. _____

8. Packages and secretes the products of the cell

8. _____

9. Involved in cell division in animal cells

9. _____

10. Fluid filled organelles enclosed by a membrane; contains stored food or wastes

10. _____

11. Site of the production of ribosomes

11. _____

12. Controls movement into and out of the nucleus

12. _____

13. Gives the cell its shape and provides protection; not found in animal cells

13. _____

14. Hairlike structures with the capacity for movement

14. _____

15. A long, hairlike structure used for movement

15. _____

16. Site of photosynthesis

16. _____

17. During cytokinesis, the new cell wall that begins to form in the middle, dividing the two sides

17. _____

18. rod-shaped bodies that carry genetic information

18. _____

PARTS OF THE CELL—MATCHING

Name _____

Match the descriptions in Column I with the name in Column II.

Column I

_____ 1. holds nucleus together

_____ 2. surface for chemical activity

_____ 3. units of heredity

_____ 4. digestion center

_____ 5. where proteins are made

_____ 6. structures involved in mitosis in animal cells only

_____ 7. microscopic cylinders that support and give the cell shape

_____ 8. shapes and supports a plant cell

_____ 9. stores and releases chemicals

_____ 10. food for plant cells is made here

_____ 11. spherical body within nucleus

_____ 12. controls entry into and out of cell

_____ 13. traps light and is used to produce food for plants

_____ 14. chromosomes are found here

_____ 15. jellylike substance within cell

_____ 16. contains code which guides all cell activities

_____ 17. minute hole in nuclear membrane

_____ 18. "powerhouse" of cell

_____ 19. contains water and dissolved minerals

_____ 20. stores food or contains pigment

Column II

a. Golgi bodies

b. nucleus

c. chromosomes

d. vacuole

e. ribosomes

f. endoplasmic reticulum

g. nuclear membrane

h. centrioles

i. cytoplasm

j. chlorophyll

k. chloroplasts

l. cell (plasma) membrane

m. cell wall

n. mitochondria

o. lysosome

p. genes

q. nuclear pore

r. nucleolus

s. plastid

t. microtubule

STAGES OF MITOSIS

Number the following six diagrams of the stages of mitosis in animal cells in the proper order. Label each stage with the proper name.

 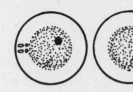 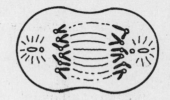

_____   _____   _____

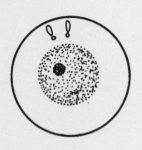  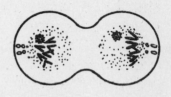

_____   _____   _____

Do the same for the following diagrams of mitosis in plant cells.

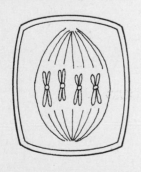  

_____   _____   _____

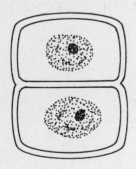 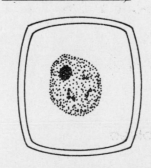 

_____   _____   _____

STAGES OF MEIOSIS

Name _____

Number the following diagrams of a first meiotic division in the proper order. Label each phase correctly as prophase I, metaphase I, anaphase I or telophase I.

 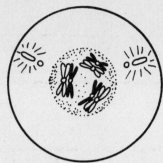  

_____   _____   _____   _____

Do the same for the diagrams of the second meiotic division. Label each phase correctly as prophase II, metaphase II, anaphase II, telophase II .

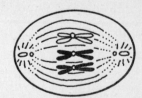

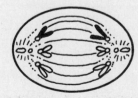

_____   _____   _____   _____   _____

COMPARING MITOSIS AND MEIOSIS

Name _____

Determine whether the following characteristics apply to mitosis, meiosis or both by putting a check in the appropriate column(s).

	Mitosis	**Meiosis**
1. no pairing of homologs occurs		
2. two divisions		
3. four daughter cells produced		
4. associated with growth and asexual reproduction		
5. associated with sexual reproduction		
6. one division		
7. two daughter cells produced		
8. involves duplication of chromosomes		
9. chromosome number is maintained		
10. chromosome number is halved		
11. crossing over between homologous chromosomes may occur		
12. daughter cells are identical to parent cell		
13. daughter cells are not identical to parent cell		
14. produces gametes		
15. synapsis occurs in prophase		

TYPES OF ASEXUAL REPRODUCTION

Name _____

Label the following diagrams of types of asexual reproduction as binary fission, budding, sporulation, regeneration, parthenogenesis or vegetative propagation. Give two examples of organisms that use each method of reproduction.

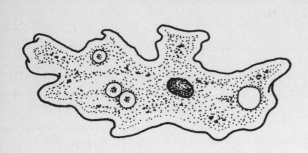

1. Type _____

   Examples _____

   _____

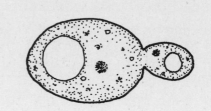

4. Type _____

   Examples _____

   _____

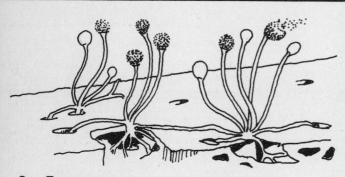

2. Type _____

   Examples _____

   _____

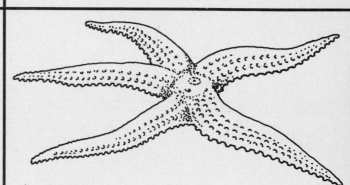

5. Type _____

   Examples _____

   _____

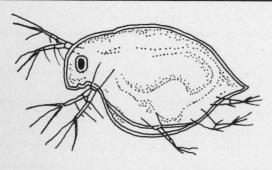

3. Type _____

   Examples _____

   _____

6. Type _____

   Examples _____

   _____

CELLULAR RESPIRATION

Name _____

Fill in the blanks in the following sequences:

Glycolysis

glucose + _____ ATP $\xrightarrow{\text{enzymes}}$ 2 _____ + _____ ATP

Anaerobic Respiration

2 pyruvic acid $\longrightarrow$ 2 _____
      or
2 pyruvic acid $\longrightarrow$ 2 _____ + 2 _____

Aerobic Respiration

2 pyruvic acid + oxygen $\xrightarrow{\text{enzymes}}$ _____ + _____ + _____ ATP

Fill in the blanks with the correct term in the questions below.

1. Glycolysis produces a net gain of _____ ATP molecules per molecule of glucose by an anaerobic reaction.

2. Aerobic respiration produces a net gain of _____ ATP molecules per molecule of glucose.

3. _____ respiration is a more efficient producer of energy than anaerobic respiration.

4. The energy contained in a molecule of glucose is changed to a more usable form by combining a _____ atom with _____ to form ATP.

5. When ATP is broken down to _____ and _____ , energy is _____ .

6. During glycolysis, glucose is first split into two molecules of _____ . This requires the energy released from two molecules of ATP being converted to two molecules of _____ .

7. The _____ is then converted to _____ , producing four _____ molecules and two _____ molecules, which are part of the electron transport chain.

8. The _____ transport chain, which supplies the energy needed for the formation of ATP, requires the formation of _____ from NAD⁺, and _____ from FAD.

9. The hydrogen necessary in this chain comes from the breaking apart of _____ molecules.

10. The oxygen released is used to form _____ .

CLASSIFICATION

Name _____

Number the seven major classification groups in order from the one containing the largest number of organisms to that containing the least.

_____ order   _____ phylum

_____ family   _____ species

_____ kingdom   _____ class

_____ genus

On the chart below, classify the five kingdoms according to the characteristic in the left-hand column.

Characteristic	Monera	Protista	Fungi	Plantae	Animalia
cell type (prokaryotic/ eukaryotic)					
number of cells (unicellular/ multicellular)					
cell nucleus (present/ absent)					
cell wall (present/ absent)					
cell wall composition					
nutrition (autotrophic/ heterotrophic)					
locomotion (present/ absent)					

CLASSIFYING ORGANISMS

The drawings below show 15 different organisms. Give the name of each organism.
Then, indicate the phylum to which it belongs.

Name _____

Phylum _____

Name _____

Phylum _____

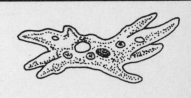

Name _____

Phylum _____

Name _____

Phylum _____

Name _____

Phylum _____

Name _____

Phylum _____

Name _____

Phylum _____

Name _____

Phylum _____

Name _____

Phylum _____

Name _____

Phylum _____

Name _____

Phylum _____

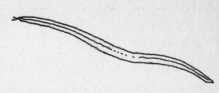

Name _____

Phylum _____

Name _____

Phylum _____

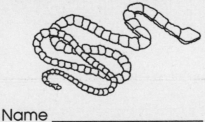

Name _____

Phylum _____

Name _____

Phylum _____

NUTRITION IN PROTOZOANS

Name _____

Label the following parts on the diagram below of an ameba. State the function/purpose of each part.

a. food vacuole _____

b. pseudopods _____

c. nucleus _____

d. contractile vacuole _____

e. cell membrane _____

f. ectoplasm _____

_____

g. endoplasm _____

_____

_____

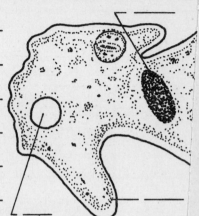
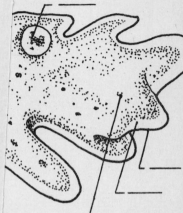

Label the following parts on the diagram below of a paramecium.

a. oral groove
b. gullet
c. anal pore
d. forming food vacuole
e. food vacuole
f. anterior contractile vacuole
g. cilia
h. micronucleus
i. macronucleus

j. pellicle
k. posterior contractile vacuole
l. mouth pore
m. trichocyst

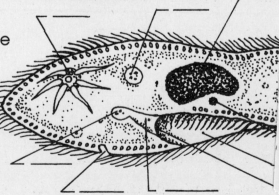

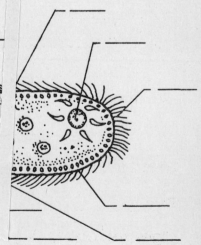

Answer the questions below.

1. Under what conditions does a paramecium discharge its trichocysts?

_____

2. How does a paramecium react if it encounters an obstacle?

_____

NUTRITION IN HYDRA

Name _____

Label the following parts of the hydra on the diagram below. State the function/purpose of each part.

a. mouth _____
   _____

b. tentacle _____
   _____

c. gastrovascular cavity _____
   _____

d. nematocysts _____
   _____

e. basal disk _____
   _____

f. egg _____
   _____

g. ovary _____
   _____

h. sperm _____
   _____

i. testis _____
   _____

j. bud _____
   _____

k. mesoglea _____
   _____

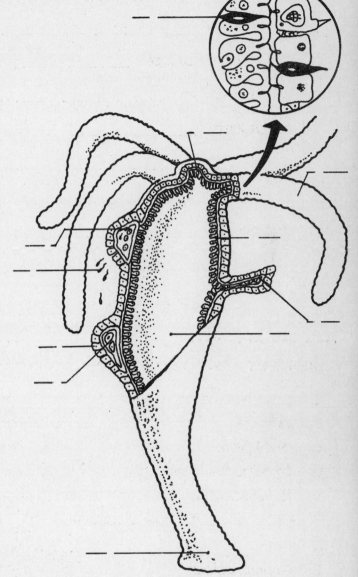

Fill in the blanks with the correct answers.

The _____ move food through the _____ into the gastrovascular, or

digestive, cavity. When the lining of the digestive cavity secretes _____ the

food is broken up into tiny pieces. The partly digested food is then engulfed by special

cells in the lining that _____ it further. Any undigested or indigestible material is

egested through the _____ .

MATCHING—CLASSIFICATION AND PROTISTS

Name _____

Match the definition in Column I with the correct word in Column II (not all words will be used).

Column I

_____ 1. method of sexual reproduction in paramecia

_____ 2. protozoan with short, hairlike structures used for movement

_____ 3. fingerlike projections of cytoplasm

_____ 4. protozoan that has a 3-stage life cycle

_____ 5. largest category in a kingdom

_____ 6. first word in a scientific name

_____ 7. science of classifying living things

_____ 8. smallest category in a kingdom

_____ 9. division of a class

_____ 10. method of reproduction in an ameba

Column II

a. pseudopod

b. genus

c. conjugation

d. slime mold

e. paramecium

f. order

g. class

h. fission

i. species

j. taxonomy

k. phylum

Match the following functions to the correct organelle.

_____ 1. gives shape to the paramecium and euglena

_____ 2. controls sexual reproduction in the paramecium

_____ 3. used for excretion of waste products

_____ 4. contains chlorophyll

_____ 5. reacts to light

_____ 6. used for movement by the euglena

_____ 7. controls metabolism of a paramecium

_____ 8. used for movement by a paramecium

_____ 9. The paramecium ingests its food through this opening.

a. cilia

b. chloroplast

c. micronucleus

d. oral groove

e. contractile vacuole

f. pellicle

g. flagellum

h. cytostome

i. eyespot

j. pseudopod

k. macronucleus

SELF QUIZ—CLASSIFICATION AND PROTISTS

Name _____

Circle the letter of the correct answer.

1. Of the following groups, a ____ contains animals that are least alike.
   a. family   b. phylum   c. division   d. class

2. Which of the following groupings contain the most closely related organisms?
   a. family   b. phylum   c. genus   d. kingdom

3. Which of the following is a correctly written scientific name?
   a. *Panthera Leo*   b. *panthera leo*   c. PANTHERA LEO   d. *Panthera leo*

4. The smallest category of a kingdom is a(n) ____ .
   a. division   b. species   c. phylum   d. genus

5. ____ is the science of classifying living things.
   a. Astronomy   b. Biology   c. Taxonomy   d. Zoology

6. The cat and dog belong to the same order but different ____ .
   a. kingdoms   b. classes   c. families   d. divisions

7. Living things are usually classified into five ____ .
   a. phyla   b. kingdoms   c. classes   d. divisions

8. Which of the following is a *Felis domesticus*?
   a. horse   b. house cat   c. house finch   d. lion

9. What language is used for scientific names?
   a. English   b. Swedish   c. German   d. Latin

10. Organisms are classified into the group with which they share the most ____ .
    a. food   b. territory   c. characteristics   d. time

11. Why does each organism have a specific scientific name?
    a. for ease of study and communication   c. name contains important information
    b. classification is less involved   d. easier to alphabetize all organisms

12. Protozoans and slime molds belong to a group of organisms known as ____ .
    a. protists   b. fungi   c. lichens   d. parasites

13. The fingerlike projections of cytoplasm used by some protozoans for movement and obtaining food are:
    a. hyphae   b. sporangia   c. pseudopods   d. oral grooves

14. A protist that has chlorophyll and produce its own food is a(n) ____ protist.
    a. plantlike   b. sporozoan   c. animallike   d. saprophyte

15. A protist covered with many, short hairlike structures used for movement is a ____ .
    a. parasite   b. ciliate   c. flagellate   d. lichen

16. Which of the following protists have shells made of silica?
    a. diatoms   b. ciliates   c. ameba   d. paramecia

17. The kingdom with one-celled organisms that are plantlike, animallike and funguslike is ____ .
    a. ameba   b. protozoa   c. protista   d. fungi

18. The long, hairlike structures protists use for locomotion are ____ .
    a. cilia   b. flagella   c. pseudopods   d. trichocysts

19. One stage of a slime mold is:
    a. stage with a hard outer shell of chitin   c. a slimy mass like an amoeba
    b. free swimming ciliate stage   d. chloroplast stage

20. *Euglena* may obtain food by making it, but *Ameba* obtains food ____ .
    a. by fermentation   b. by surrounding it   c. along an oral groove   d. from a host

SELF QUIZ—VIRUSES

Name _____

Fill in the blanks from the word list below.

AIDS	antibodies	cells	interferon
measles	mumps	protein	reproduction
	vaccines	weakened	

1. Viruses consist of nucleic acids covered by a coat of _____ .

2. Viruses, unlike bacteria, are not composed of _____ .

3. The only life function viruses can perform is _____ .

4. Protection against some viral diseases can be produced by _____ .

5. Name three viral diseases: _____ , _____ and
   _____ .

6. A vaccine is made from a _____ form of the virus.

7. Two natural defenses the body has against viruses are _____ and
   _____ .

Below are diagrams of three different types of viruses. Label the nucleic acid and protein coat in the polyhedral and rod-shaped viruses. Label the capsid, collar, tail sheath, tail fiber and base plate in the bacteriophage.

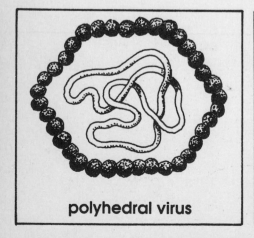

polyhedral virus

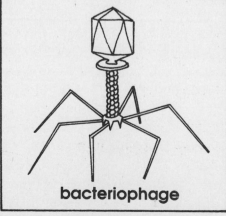

bacteriophage

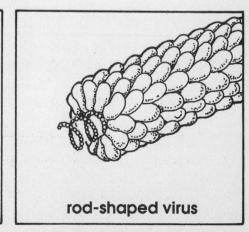

rod-shaped virus

BACTERIA—TYPICAL MONERANS

Name _____

Structure of Bacteria

Label the parts of a moneran on the diagram below. State the function/purpose of each.

a. flagella _____

b. ribosomes _____

c. nucleoid _____
   _____

d. cell wall _____
   _____

e. cell (plasma) membrane _____
   _____

f. capsule _____
   _____

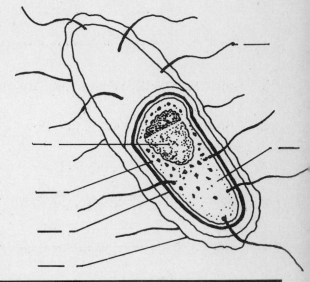

Conjugation in Bacteria

The diagrams below show conjugation, a means of genetic transfer but not reproduction in bacteria. During conjugation, a plasmid is transferred from a donor to a recipient bacterium. Label the donor bacterium, the recipient bacterium, the plasmid and the cytoplasmic bridge on the diagrams.

Answer the questions below.

1. By what process do bacteria reproduce?

   _____

2. What structures do some bacteria form under unfavorable conditions?

   _____

3. What do the monerans lack in their cell structure that is present in most other organisms? _____

4. Are the monerans prokaryotic or eukaryotic?

   _____

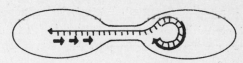
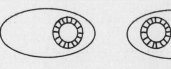
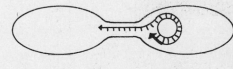
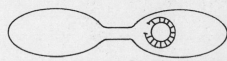
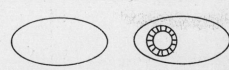

SELF QUIZ—MONERANS

Name _____

Put the correct answer to the questions in the blanks using the words from the list below.

1. Monerans have no definite _____ , but can still carry on reproduction.

2. Monerans have no _____ , but can still carry on cellular respiration.

3. Cyanobacteria may also be called _____ .

4. When cyanobacterial multiply rapidly in a pond, they use up all the _____ .

5. Bacteria come in what three shapes? _____ , _____ ,
   _____

6. Some bacteria have a whiplike tail called a _____ .

7. Bacteria that do not need oxygen to live are called _____ .

8. Bacteria reproduce by what process? _____

9. Bacteria that live on dead organic matter are called _____ .

10. Relationship between two organisms that do not harm either one is
    _____

11. Two conditions bacteria need to live: _____ , _____

12. Four ways we have of controlling bacterial growth. _____
    _____

13. _____ are the oldest known and simplest organism.

14. _____ bacteria live in nodules on the roots of plants, fixing
    atmospheric nitrogen, thus making it available for their own metabolic activities.

15. _____ is the most important source of variability in bacteria.

16. Many scientists have suggested that _____ should be considered a
    separate kingdom because they are remarkably different from all the bacteria.

17. _____ are the source of a majority, over 2000 kinds, of antibiotics.

18. _____ are the causative agents of syphilis and Lyme disease.

19. _____ bacteria depend on chemical sources—ammonia, methane
    and hydrogen sulfide—for energy for their metabolism.

20. _____ were probably responsible for the accumulation of limestone
    deposits known as stromatolites.

actinomycetes	anaerobes	archaebacteria	binary fission	bacteria
blue-green algae	canning	chemosynthetic	cyanobactyeria	flagellum
freezing	mitochondria	moisture	mutation	mutualism
nitrogen fixing	nucleus	oxygen	proper temperature	radiation
refrigeration	round rodlike	saprophytes	spiral	spirochetes

42

THREE TYPES OF FUNGI

Label the following parts on the diagram of a mushroom below.

a. cap
b. gills
c. stipe
d. basidia
e. rhizoids

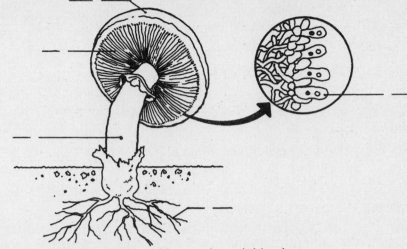

Label the following parts on the diagram of bread mold below.

a. sporangia
b. spores
c. sporangiophore
d. stolon
e. rhizoid

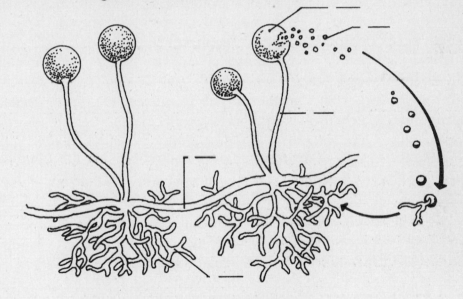

Label the following parts on the diagram of a yeast cell below.

a. bud
b. cell wall
c. nucleus
d. vacuole
e. cytoplasm

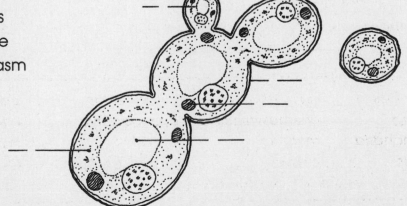

SELF QUIZ—FUNGI

Name _____

Circle the letter of the correct answer.

1. During the process of ____ energy is released.
   - a. parasitism
   - b. fermentation
   - c. mutualism
   - d. reproduction

2. ____ are saclike structures that produce many spores.
   - a. Pseudopods
   - b. Gilia
   - c. Sporangia
   - d. Hyphae

3. Club fungi produce spores on a sac called a(n) ____ .
   - a. bud
   - b. basidium
   - c. ascus
   - d. stripe

4. Bread mold produces masses of threadlike structures called ____ .
   - a. flagella
   - b. cilia
   - c. hyphae
   - d. pseudopods

5. ____ are fungi that produce spores in special structures on the tips of hyphae.
   - a. Yeasts
   - b. Lichens
   - c. Mushrooms
   - d. Sporangia fungi

6. ____ is a type of sexual reproduction in which an outgrowth from the parent organism forms a new organism.
   - a. Budding
   - b. Zygospore
   - c. Sporangia
   - d. Basidia

7. Sac fungi are fungi that ____ .
   - a. look like mosses
   - b. are one-celled
   - c. are helpful because they produce enzymes
   - d. produce spores inside an ascus

8. Yeast cells may reproduce by forming spores or by ____ .
   - a. fermentation
   - b. budding
   - c. respiration
   - d. dehydration

9. A sporangium fungus obtains food by ____ .
   - a. respiration
   - b. dehydration
   - c. absorption
   - d. mutualism

10. Club fungi include puffballs, bracken fungi and __ .
    - a. molds
    - b. yeasts
    - c. mushrooms
    - d. lichens

11. A sporangium fungus reproduces by ____ .
    - a. budding and spores
    - b. spores and zygospores
    - c. anaerobic respiration
    - d. a micronucleus

12. Unlike a plant, a fungus does not have ____ .
    - a. very many cells
    - b. chlorophyll
    - c. cell walls
    - d. buds

13. Which one of the following helpful fungi is used to flavor cheese?
    - a. mushrooms
    - b. saprophytic fungi
    - c. yeast
    - d. molds

14. Each basidium will produce how many spores?
    - a. thousands
    - b. hundreds
    - c. four
    - d. ten

15. The basidia are found on what part of the mushroom?
    - a. stipe
    - b. gills
    - c. cap
    - d. hyphae

16. Fermentation produces what products?
    - a. alcohol and carbon dioxide
    - b. air bubbles and sugar
    - c. alcohol and water
    - d. carbon dioxide and sugar

17. Masses of hyphae are called ____ .
    - a. basidia
    - b. sporangia
    - c. mycelium
    - d. asci

18. Another name for anaerobic respiration in fungi is ____ .
    - a. budding
    - b. reproduction
    - c. breathing
    - d. fermentation

19. A person who studies fungi is called a ____ .
    - a. fungicide
    - b. mycologist
    - c. zygospore
    - d. saprophyte

20. The cell walls of fungi are made of ____ .
    - a. cellulose
    - b. chitin
    - c. silica
    - d. tissue

CROSS SECTION OF A LEAF

Name _____

Label the following parts of the leaf in the diagram below. Give the purpose/function of each part.

a. lower epidermis _____

b. upper epidermis _____

c. palisade layer _____

d. cuticle _____

e. stomate _____

f. guard cells _____

g. vein (fibrovascular bundle) _____

h. spongy layer _____

i. air space _____

j. xylem _____

k. phloem _____

l. chloroplasts _____

m. mesophyll _____

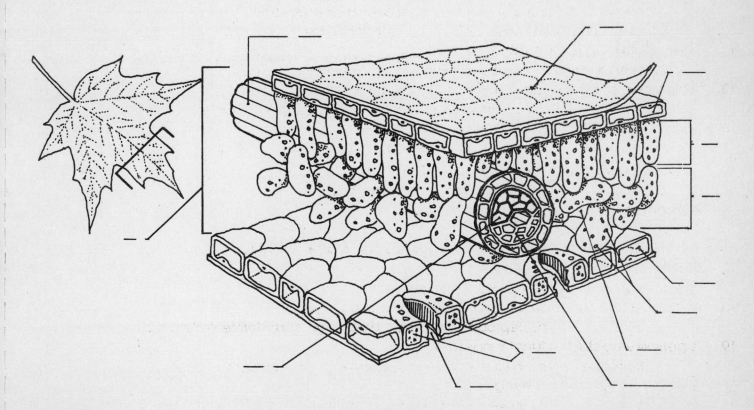

LEAF CROSSWORD

Name _____

Across

3. outermost cellular layer of the leaf
5. where most photosynthesis takes place in the leaf
8. carry food and water to the cells
10. food-making process occurring in leaves
11. gas necessary for photosynthesis
12. green pigment necessary for photosynthesis

Down

1. control the size of the stoma opening
2. allow the exchange of gases between the environment and the air spaces inside the leaf
4. organelles that contain chlorophyll
6. beneath the palisade layer
7. end product of photosynthesis
9. waxy coat of the leaf

STRUCTURE OF A ROOT

Name _____

Label the following parts on the diagrams of a cross-section and longitudinal section of a root below.

a. xylem
b. phloem
c. vascular cylinder
d. epidermis
e. foot hair
f. root cap
g. cortex
h. pericycle
i. cambium
j. region of differentiation
k. region of elongation
l. region of meristematic growth

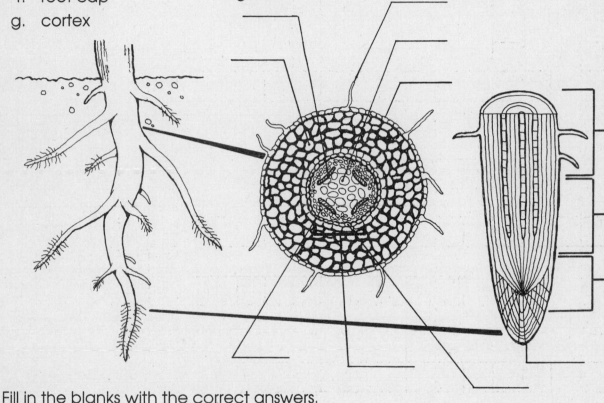

Fill in the blanks with the correct answers.

The end of the root that absorbs minerals and _____ is the

_____. The root tip is protected by several layers of cells called the

_____. In the region of _____, cells mature and become

specialized in function. Some cells in the outer layer develop _____. These

_____ are elongated cells that increase the surface area of the root to

maximize absorption of _____ and minerals from the _____.

The _____ and vascular cylinder are separated by the _____.

In the vascular cylinder, the xylem and _____ are separated by the

_____.

STRUCTURE OF A FLOWER

Name _____

Label the parts of the flower in the diagram below. Give the purpose/function of each part.

a. ovary _____

b. style _____

c. stigma _____

d. sepal _____

e. receptacle _____

f. pedicel _____

g. petal _____

h. filament _____

i. anther _____

j. pollen grain _____

_____

k. pistil _____

_____

l. stamen _____

_____

m. ovule _____

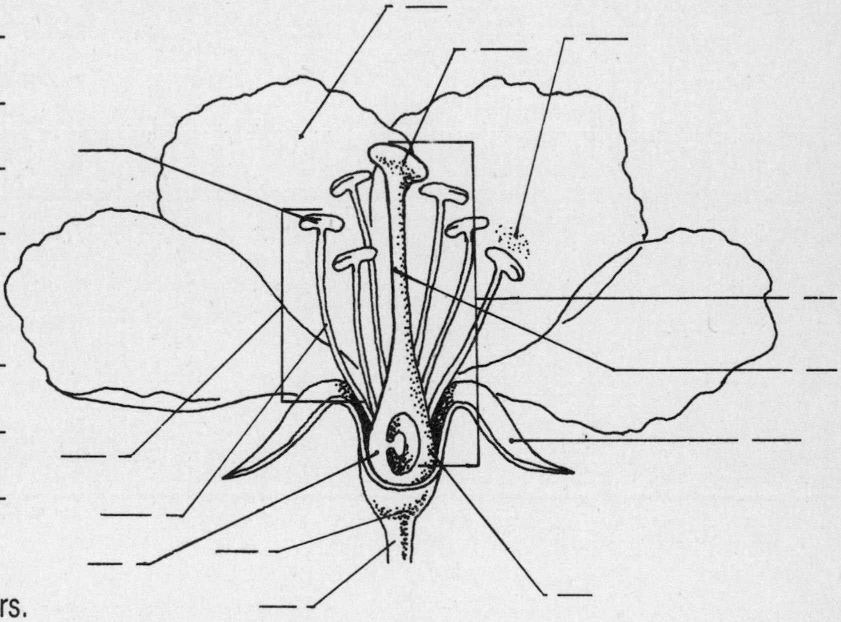

_____

Fill in the blanks with the correct answers.

If there are to be more flowers, _____ must take place. In pollination, pollen

is transferred from the _____ to the _____. In detail, pollen is

transferred from the _____ of the stamen to the _____ of the

pistil. In some flowers, pollen falls on the stigma of the _____ flower.

_____-pollination occurs. In other flowers, pollen from _____

flower falls on the stigma of a _____ flower. _____-

pollination takes place.

48

©Instructional Fair, Inc.

STRUCTURE OF THE STAMEN AND A POLLEN GRAIN

Name _____

Label the following parts on the diagrams of double fertilization in the flower below.

a. anther
b. filament
c. pollen grain
d. generative nucleus
e. sperm nuclei
f. tube nucleus

g. pollen tube
h. stigma
i. style
j. ovary
k. ovule
l. embryo sac

m. egg
n. micropyle
o. polar nuclei
p. endosperm nucleus
q. fertilized egg

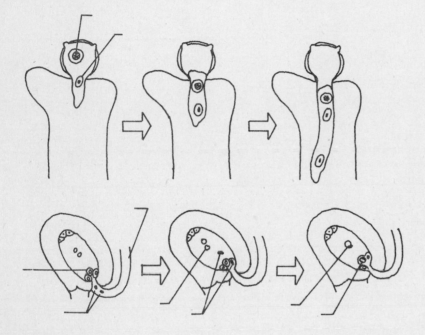
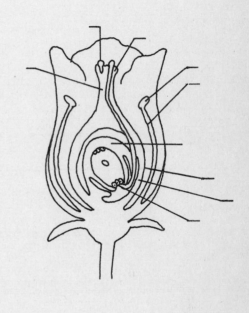

Fill in the blanks.

Each pollen grain contains 2 sperm nuclei, one is a _____ nucleus and the other a _____ nucleus. After pollination, the pollen grain that falls on the _____ begins to form a _____ , probably under the control of the _____ nucleus. The pollen tube grows through the _____ into the ovary. The _____ nucleus moves down the _____ where it divides into _____ sperm nuclei. Inside the embryo sac, one _____ nucleus joins with the _____ nucleus, producing a fertilized _____ . This is the process of _____ . The second _____ nucleus joins with the _____ nuclei to form an _____ nucleus, which develops into the _____ .

METAMORPHOSIS

Name _____

As insects develop they undergo metamorphosis, a series of definite changes in appearance. Some insects, such as a butterfly, undergo complete metamorphosis. Other insects, such as the grasshopper, undergo incomplete metamorphosis.

Label the four stages on the diagram of the complete metamorphosis of the butterfly at the left below.

Label the three stages on the diagram of the incomplete metamorphosis of the grasshopper at the right below.

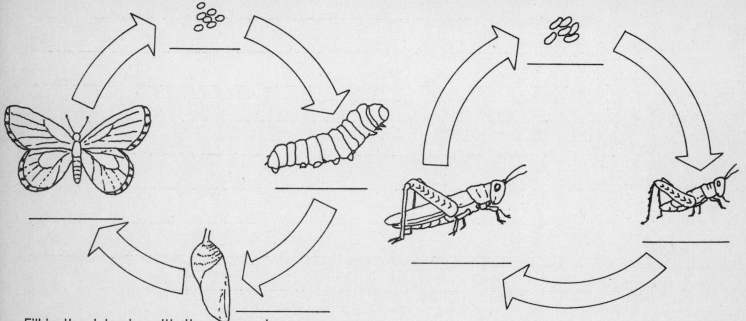

Complete Metamorphosis   Incomplete Metamorphosis

Fill in the blanks with the correct answers.

In complete metamorphosis, a female butterfly hatches into a wormlike organism called a _____ or caterpillar. During this stage, the organism consumes a large amount of food. The _____ or caterpillar then spins a protective covering around itself and becomes a _____ or chrysalis. This covering is called a _____ . While inside this covering, the _____ changes into an _____ .

In _____ metamorphosis, a grasshopper goes through a _____ change from egg to _____ . The grasshopper begins as an _____ and hatches into a _____ . A nymph is an immature _____ that resembles a full-grown grasshopper but lacks _____ . As the nymph grows, it _____ until it reaches the last stage, the _____ .

STRUCTURE OF A BIRD'S EGG

Name _____

Label the parts of the newly fertilized bird's egg and the developing bird's egg in the diagrams below. State the purpose/function of each part.

a. shell _____

b. amnion _____

c. amniotic fluid _____

d. embryo _____

e. chorion _____

f. yolk sac _____

g. blood vessels _____

h. allantois _____

i. albumin _____

j. air space _____

k. shell membrane _____

l. yolk _____

m. chalaza _____

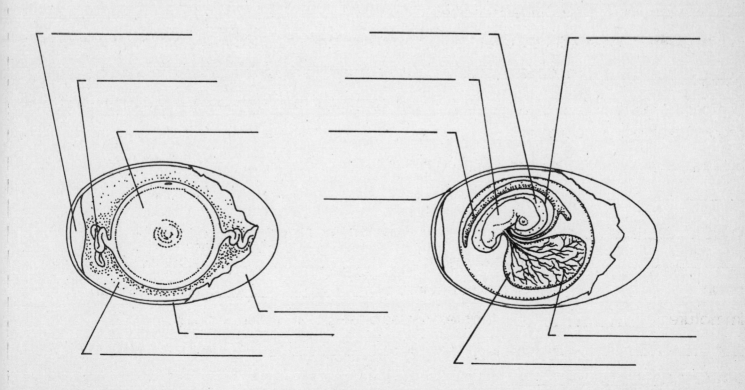

PUNNETT SQUARES—
CROSSES INVOLVING ONE TRAIT

Name _____

In a certain species of animal, black fur (B) is dominant over brown fur (b). Using the following Punnett square, predict the genotypes and phenotypes of the offspring whose parents are both Bb or have heterozygous black fur.

Genotypes: _____% homozygous black fur (BB)

_____% heterozygous black fur (Bb)

_____% homozygous brown fur (bb)

Phenotypes: _____% black fur

_____% brown fur

Now do the same when one parent is homozygous black and the other is homozygous brown.

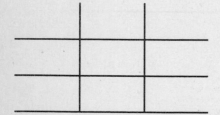

Genotypes: _____% homozygous black fur (BB)

_____% heterozygous black fur (Bb)

_____% homozygous brown fur (bb)

Phenotypes: _____% black fur

_____% brown fur

Repeat this process again when one parent is heterozygous black and the other is homozygous brown.

Genotypes: _____% homozygous black fur (BB)

_____% heterozygous black fur (Bb)

_____% homozygous brown fur (bb)

Phenotypes: _____% black fur

_____% brown fur

BLOOD TYPE AND INHERITANCE

Name _____

In blood typing, the gene for type A and the gene for type B are codominant. The gene for type O is recessive. Using Punnett squares, determine the possible blood types of the offspring when:

1. Father is type O, Mother is type O

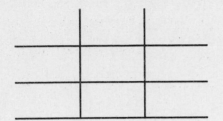

_____% O
_____% A
_____% B
_____% AB

2. Father is type A, homozygous; Mother is type B, homozygous

_____% O
_____% A
_____% B
_____% AB

3. Father is type A, heterozygous; Mother is type B, heterozygous

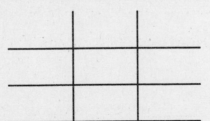

_____% O
_____% A
_____% B
_____% AB

4. Father is type O, Mother is type AB

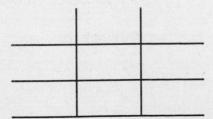

_____% O
_____% A
_____% B
_____% AB

5. Father and Mother are both type AB

_____% O
_____% A
_____% B
_____% AB

PUNNETT SQUARES—
CROSSES INVOLVING TWO TRAITS

Name _____

In a dihybrid cross, when two traits are considered, the number of possible combinations in the offspring increases. Suppose that black hair (B) is dominant over blonde hair (b) and brown eyes (E) are dominant over blue eyes (e).

What percent of offspring could be expected to have blonde hair and blue eyes if:

1. The father has black hair (heterozygous) and brown eyes (heterozygous) and the mother has blonde hair and blue eyes.

    Genotype of father—BbEe

    Genotype of mother—bbee

    In the Punnett square below, complete the remaining gametes of the father. Then, fill in the boxes below.

	BE	Be		
be				

_____%

2. Both parents have black hair (heterozygous) and brown eyes (heterozygous).

    Genotype of father— _____

    Genotype of Mother— _____

    Complete the Punnett square below.

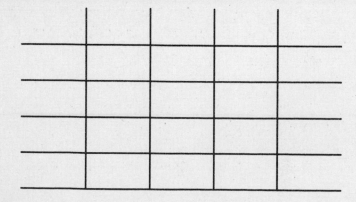

_____%

In each dihybrid cross, the phenotype ratio of individuals with brown hair and brown eyes, brown hair and blue eyes, blonde hair and brown eyes and blonde hair and blue eyes is

_____ : _____ : _____ : _____

HUMAN PEDIGREES

Name _____

By studying a human pedigree, you can determine whether a trait is dominant or recessive. To interpret the three pedigrees below, use the same key shown at the right. Of course, the individual with the trait could be homozygous dominant or heterozygous dominant.

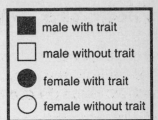

■ male with trait
□ male without trait
● female with trait
○ female without trait

A. The pedigree shows the inheritance of attached earlobes for four generations.

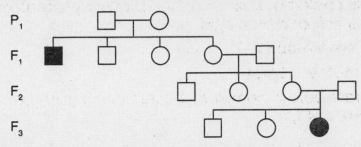

Is the trait for attached earlobes, versus free earlobes, dominant or recessive?
_____ How do you know? _____
_____

B. The pedigree shows the inheritance of tongue rolling.

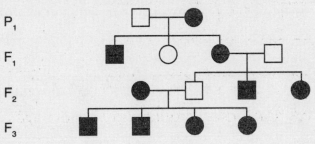

Is this trait dominant or recessive? _____ Explain. _____
_____
_____

C. This pedigree shows the inheritance of colorblindness, a sex-linked trait.

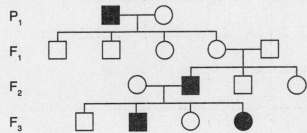

Is this trait dominant or recessive? _____ Is the mother of the colorblind girl in the F_3 generation colorblind, a carrier, or a person with normal color vision?
_____ Explain. _____
_____

DNA MOLECULE AND REPLICATION

Name _____

The building blocks of the DNA molecule are nucleotides, which consist of a phosphate, a deoxyribose sugar and a nitrogenous base. In the diagram, label these three substances on the nucleotide. The letters representing the four different nitrogeneous bases are shown in the nucleotides at the right. Place the name of the base next to its letter symbol in the appropriate space.

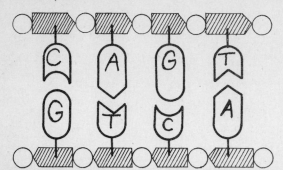

A = _____

T = _____

G = _____

C = _____

The DNA molecule has a double helix shape. Two strands of DNA are coiled around each other and attached by bonds between the nitrogenous bases of each chain. Adenine always bonds with thymine, and cytosine bonds with guanine.

In the illustration at the left below, label a phosphate and a deoxyribose sugar. Fill in the symbol for each base depending on its complementary base in the opposite strand.

The diagram at the right shows the replication of DNA. Fill in the symbol for each base. Label the original strand, a new strand and a free-floating nucleotide.

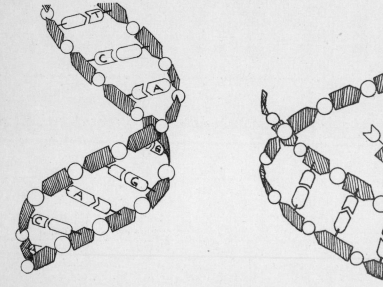
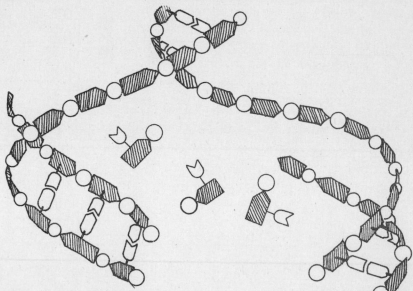

Fill in the blanks with the correct answers.

The structure of DNA was determined by _____ and _____ .

They described the shape of the DNA molecule as a _____ .

After replication, _____ identical molecules of _____ are

produced. A gene is a sequence of _____ in a DNA molecule.

©Instructional Fair, Inc.

mRNA AND TRANSCRIPTION

Name _____

Transcription

Fill in the blanks below. On the illustration of transcription, label the DNA, the newly-forming mRNA, the completed strand of mRNA and a free nucleotide.

Messenger RNA (mRNA) carries the instructions to make a

particular _____ from the DNA in the

_____ to the ribosomes. The process of

producing mRNA from instructions in the DNA is called

_____.

During transcription, the DNA molecule unwinds and

separates, exposing the nitrogenous bases. Free RNA

_____ pair with the exposed bases. There is

no _____ (T) in RNA. _____ (U)

pairs with adenine (A) instead. RNA contains the sugar

_____ instead of deoxyribose. The mRNA

molecule is completed by the formation of

_____ between the RNA

_____, and it then separates from the DNA.

The mRNA molecule is a _____ strand, unlike

DNA.

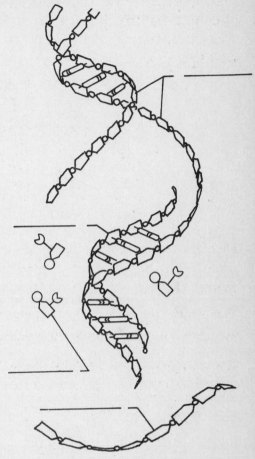

Codons

Each combination of three nitrogenous bases on the mRNA molecule is a codon, a three-letter code word for a specific amino acid.
The table below shows the mRNA codon for each amino acid. Use the table to answer the questions below.

1. The codon for trytophan is _____.

2. For leucine, there are _____ different codons.

3. The codon GAU is for

   _____.

4. In a stop codon, if the second base is G, the first and third bases are _____ and _____.

	Second Base in Code Word				
	A	**G**	**U**	**C**	
A	Lysine	Arginine	Isoleucine	Threonine	A
	Lysine	Arginine	Methionine	Threonine	G
	Asparagine	Serine	Isoleucine	Threonine	U
	Asparagine	Serine	Isoleucine	Threonine	C
G	Glutamic Acid	Glycine	Valine	Alanine	A
	Glutamic Acid	Glycine	Valine	Alanine	G
	Aspartic Acid	Glycine	Valine	Alanine	U
	Aspartic Acid	Glycine	Valine	Alanine	C
U	"Stop" codon	"Stop" codon	Leucine	Serine	A
	"Stop" codon	Trytophan	Leucine	Serine	G
	Tyrosine	Cysteine	Phenylalanine	Serine	U
	Tyrosine	Cysteine	Phenylalanine	Serine	C
C	Glutamine	Arginine	Leucine	Proline	A
	Glutamine	Arginine	Leucine	Proline	G
	Histidine	Arginine	Leucine	Proline	U
	Histidine	Arginine	Leucine	Proline	C

First Base in Code Word (left) · Third Base in Code Word (right)

GENETICS CROSSWORD

Name _____

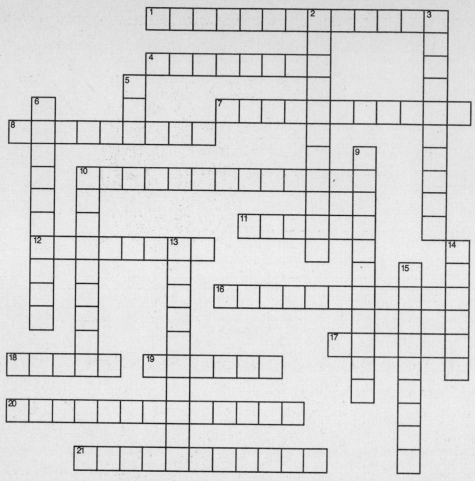

Across

1. Occurs when a segment of chromosome breaks off and becomes reattached to another chromosome
4. An organism that is heterozygous for two traits
7. Humans have 46 of these.
8. Capacity of one allele to suppress the expression of a contrasting, recessive gene
10. Diagram used to predict the results of genetic crosses
11. This base is found in RNA, but not in DNA
12. Genetic makeup of an individual
16. Assembly of a protein molecule according to the code in a mRNA molecule
17. The sugar in RNA
18. Found on chromosomes, they determine specific characteristics of the organism
19. Different form of a gene
20. The process of producing mRNA from instructions in DNA
21. Sugar in DNA

Down

2. Occurs when both alleles are equally dominant
3. Subunit of DNA consisting of a nitrogenous base, a sugar and a phosphate group
5. Double helix in which the genetic code is found
6. Two dominant or two recessive genes for the same trait
9. Process by which DNA makes an exact copy of itself
10. Appearance of an individual due to its genetic makeup
13. Presence of complete extra sets of chromosomes
14. Conducted experiments on heredity in pea plants
15. Site of protein synthesis

UROGENITAL SYSTEM OF A FROG

Name _____

Label the following parts of the urinary and reproductive systems of a female frog.

a. fat bodies
b. oviduct
c. egg mass
d. adrenal gland
e. ureter
f. uteri
g. kidney
h. cloaca
i. urinary bladder

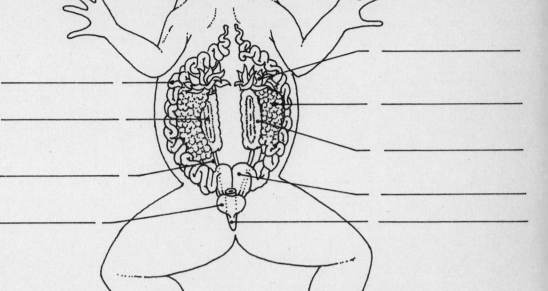

Label the following parts of the urinary and reproductive systems of a male frog.

a. fat bodies
b. testes
c. adrenal gland
d. ureter
e. vestigial oviduct
f. kidney
g. cloaca
h. urinary bladder

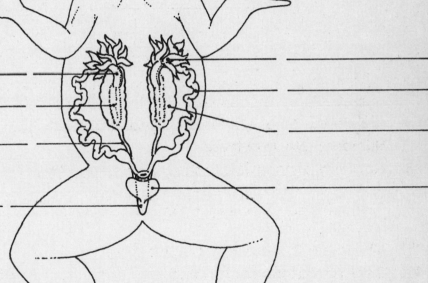

Fill in the blanks with the correct answers.

In the female, in the spring the _____ become large with _____ .

When the eggs are laid, they travel through the _____ into the

_____ . The male deposits _____ , which are produced in the

_____ and travel out the _____ , over the _____

as they are being laid in the water.

THE EARTHWORM

Name _____

Digestive System

Label the following parts of the digestive system of the earthworm.

a. crop
b. esophagus
c. intestine
d. mouth
e. anus
f. gizzard

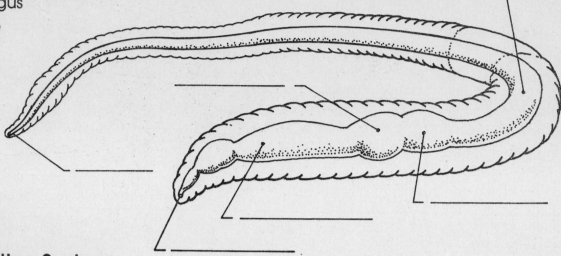

Reproductive System

Label the following parts of the reproductive system of the earthworm.

a. sperm receptacle
b. testis
c. sperm reservoir
d. ovary
e. clitellum

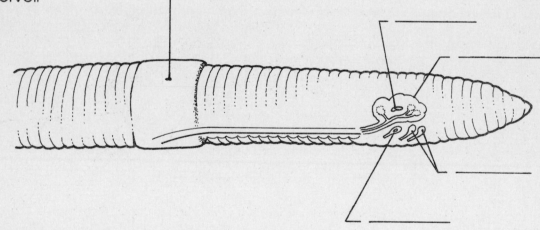

Fill in the blanks with the correct answers.

In the earthworm, after food enters the mouth, it passes through the _____ and

is then stored in the _____. From there, it passes to the _____,

where it is mechanically broken down by grinding. After this, it is chemically broken down

in the _____. Undigested material is egested through the _____.

Since an earthworm produces both eggs and sperm, it is considered to be a

_____. However, an earthworm _____ self-fertilize.

THE GRASSHOPPER

Name _____

External Anatomy

Label the following parts of the external anatomy of the grasshopper.

a. antenna
b. simple eye
c. compound eye
d. ear
e. legs
f. wings
g. egg-laying apparatus
h. spiracles

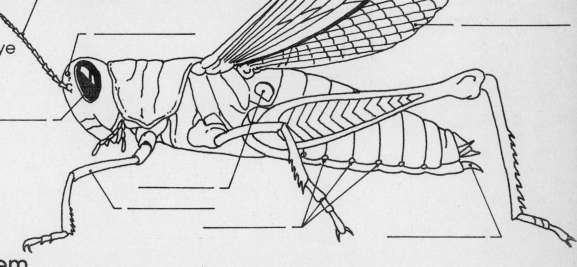

Digestive System

Label the following parts of the digestive system of the grasshopper.

a. crop
b. gizzard
c. stomach
d. intestine
e. mouth
f. anus
g. gastric caeca
h. salivary glands
i. rectum

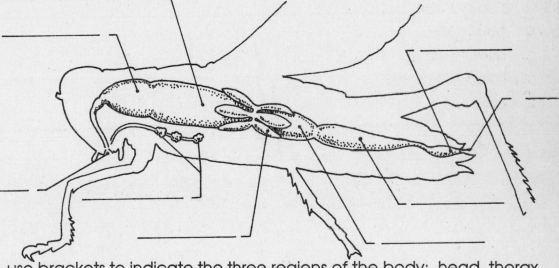

On the top diagram, use brackets to indicate the three regions of the body: head, thorax and abdomen.

Fill in the blanks with the correct answers.

The grasshopper ingests food through the _____. The food is temporarily

stored in the _____, after which it passes to the _____ for

mechanical grinding. Digestion takes place in the _____ and

_____. Undigested waste is egested through the _____. On its

thorax, a grasshopper has _____ pairs of _____ legs and _____

pairs of wings. The _____ on the abdomen are used to carry oxygen.

61

THE FROG—PART I

Digestive System

Label the following parts of
the digestive system of a frog.

a. mouth
b. esophagus
c. liver
d. gall bladder
e. pancreas
f. stomach
g. small intestine
h. large intestine
i. cloaca
j. anus

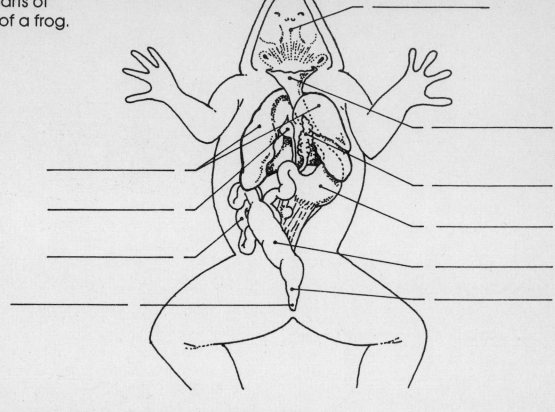

Skeletal System

Label the following parts of the skeletal system of a frog.

a. skull
b. shoulder blade
c. collarbone
d. humerus
e. radio-ulna
f. vertebrae
g. breastbone
h. pelvic girdle
i. femur
j. knee
k. tibio-fibula
l. ankle bone
m. bones of feet

CIRCULATORY SYSTEMS

Name _____

Label the following parts of the circulatory system of the earthworm in the diagram.

   a. aortic arches
   b. ventral blood vessel
   c. dorsal blood vessel

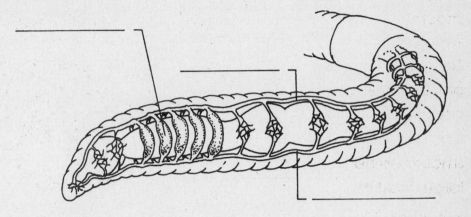

Label the following parts of the circulatory system of the grasshopper.

   a. aorta
   b. sinuses
   c. heart

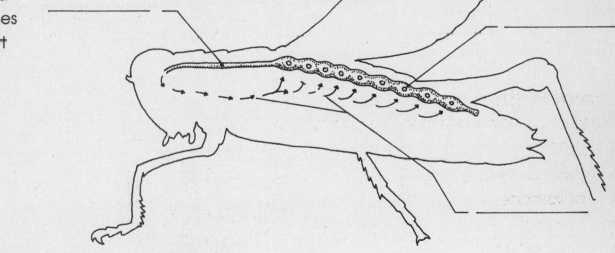

Fill in the blanks with the correct answers.

1. Which organism has an open circulatory system? _____

2. Which organism has a closed circulatory system? _____

3. Which type of blood vessel is the aorta? _____

4. In the earthworm, the aortic arches act as _____.

5. In the earthworm, blood flows from the _____ blood vessel to the
     _____ blood vessel.

6. In a grasshopper, blood re-enters the heart through several pairs of ostia, or
     _____.

GAS EXCHANGE IN LIVING ORGANISMS

Name _____

Fill in the blanks with the correct answers.

1. In the simplest organisms, where the outer membrane of the organism is in direct contact with the environment, the exchange of gases occurs by the process of _____ .

2. In plants, the exchange of gases occur mainly through the _____ and _____ .

3. In the hydra, gas exchange occurs directly between the water and the cells through the process of _____ .

4. In the earthworm, the exchange of gases occurs through the _____ .

5. Label the following parts of the respiratory system of the grasshopper on the diagram.

   a. air sacs
   b. tracheal tubes
   c. spiracles

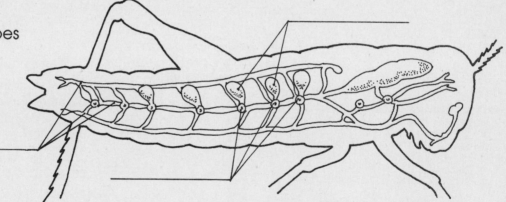

6. Label the following parts of the respiratory system of the frog on the diagram.

   a. lungs _____
   b. skin
   c. nostrils _____
   d. mouth

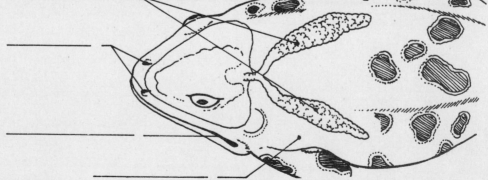

7. Openings in the grasshopper's body by which gases enter and leave are the _____ .

8. These openings are attached to _____ which deliver and receive gases at the moist membranes of the animal's internal tissues.

EXCRETION IN LIVING ORGANISMS

Name _____

Fill in the blanks with the correct answers.

1. In one-celled organisms and plants, excess water or toxic substances can be contained in _____ . Specialized types of these organelles, called _____ _____ , can expel these substances from the cell.

2. In the hydra, metabolic waste products are discharged directly into the _____. Gases are also exchanged between the cells and the _____.

3. Label the following parts of the excretory system of the earthworm on the diagram.
    a. nephridium
    b. excretory pore
    c. tubule

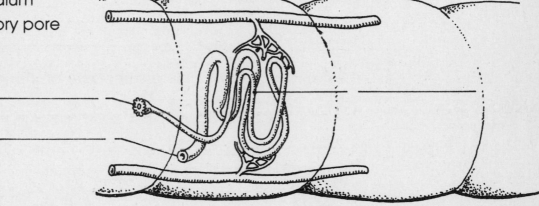

4. Label the following parts of the excretory system of the grasshopper on the diagram.
    a. Malpighian tubules
    b. rectum
    c. intestine
    d. anus

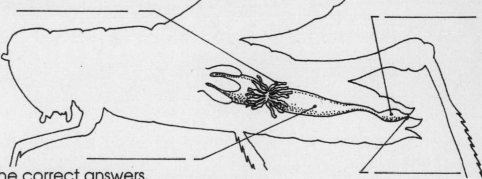

Fill in the blanks with the correct answers.

In the earthworm, water, mineral salts and urea are filtered out of the body fluids into the _____ , and are then excreted. There are _____ nephridia in most of the body segments. Each nephridium does the same job as the _____ in a human. The sites in the grasshopper in which water, mineral salts and uric acid accumulate are called _____. These tubules remove cell wastes from the _____ and pass them into the _____. From here they are eliminated from the body along with the _____ wastes.

NERVOUS SYSTEMS OF THE EARTHWORM AND GRASSHOPPER

Name _____

Label the following parts of the nervous system of the earthworm on the diagram below.

a. brain
b. nerves
c. ventral nerve cord
d. ganglia

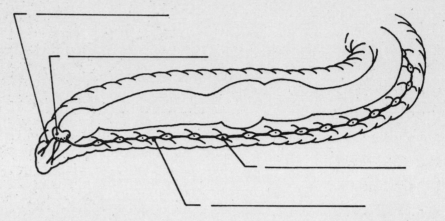

Label the following parts of the nervous system of the grasshopper on the diagram below.

a. brain
b. antennae
c. compound eye
d. nerves
e. ventral nerve cord
f. ganglia

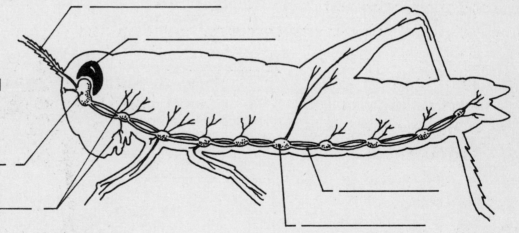

Fill in the blanks with the correct answers.

In the earthworm, two nerves from the paired _____ run around each side

of the _____ to the _____ side of the worm. Here they join to

become a double _____ cord which runs to the last segment. In each

_____, they join to become an enlarged _____.

In the grasshopper, the most prominent parts of the brain are the _____

lobes. The large _____ eyes are made up of many _____ so

the grasshopper can see in many directions at the same time. The _____

nerve cord contains many _____. The largest ganglion sends messages to

the _____ legs.

THE FROG—PART II

Name _____

Nervous System

Label the following parts of the nervous system of a frog.

a. olfactory lobe
b. cerebrum
c. optic lobe
d. cerebellum
e. medulla oblongata
f. cranial nerves
g. spinal cord
h. spinal nerves
i. brachial nerve
j. sciatic nerve
k. chain of autonomic ganglia

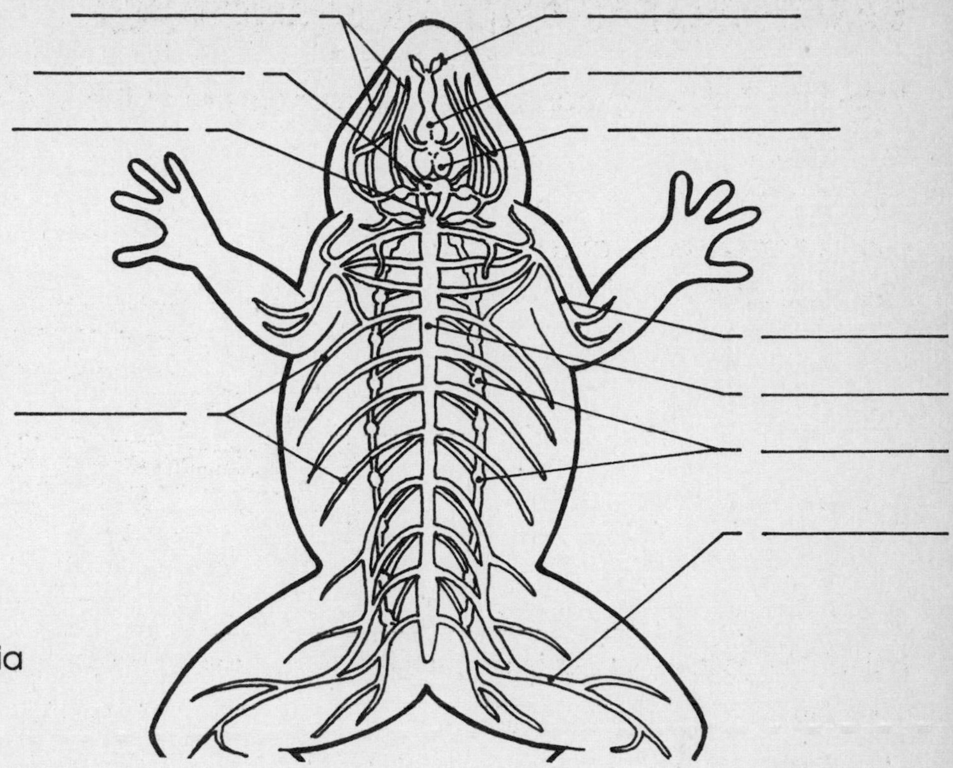

Circulatory System

Label the following parts of the circulatory system of a frog.

a. left atrium
b. right atrium
c. ventricle
d. pulmonary artery
e. vein from head
f. artery to head
g. vein from leg
h. artery to leg

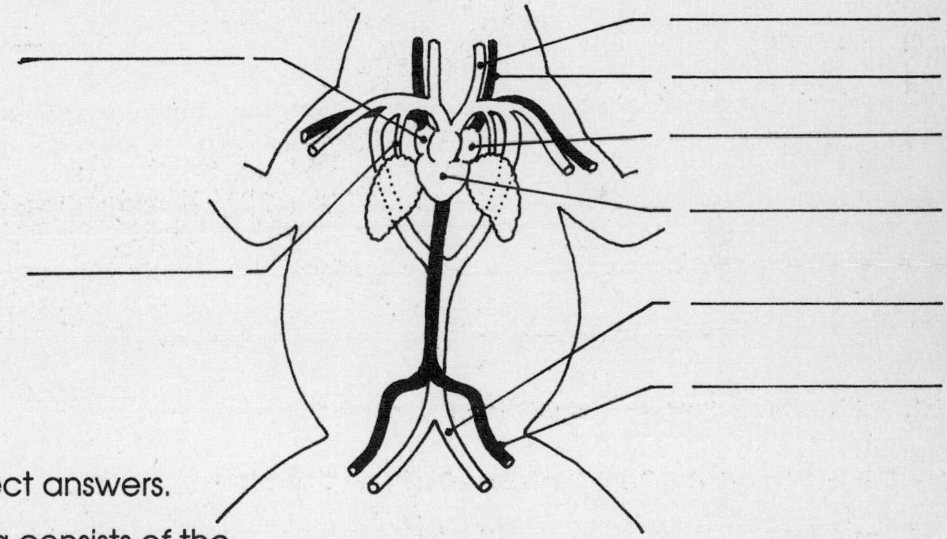

Fill in the blanks with the correct answers.

The nervous system of the frog consists of the _____, _____

and nerves. The _____ lobes lie at the anterior end of the brain. Behind

these are the lobes of the _____. Next are the _____ lobes,

behind which are the _____ and _____.

The heart of a frog, unlike the heart of a human, has _____ ventricle. Blood

flows from the left _____ to the ventricle, around the body and back to the

_____ atrium. From there, it flows to the _____ and then to

the left _____.

STRUCTURE OF A STARFISH

Name _____

Label the following parts of a starfish on the diagram below. Give the purpose/function of each part.

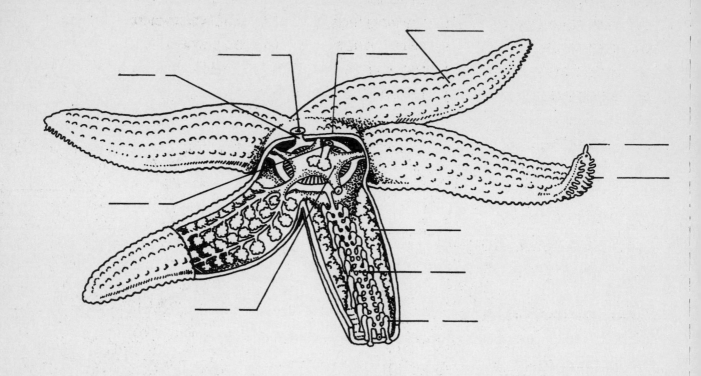

a. arm _____

b. sieve plate _____

c. stomach _____

d. anus _____

e. tube feet _____

f. ring canal _____

g. stone canal _____

h. radial canal _____

i. ampulla _____

j. gonad _____

k. eyespot _____

STRUCTURE OF A CRAYFISH

Name _____

Label the following parts of the crayfish on the diagrams of the dorsal and/or ventral views below.

a. carapace
b. compound eye
c. antennule
d. mandible
e. cheliped

f. antenna
g. walking legs
h. swimmerets
i. uropod
j. telson

k. anus
l. cephalothorax
m. abdomen

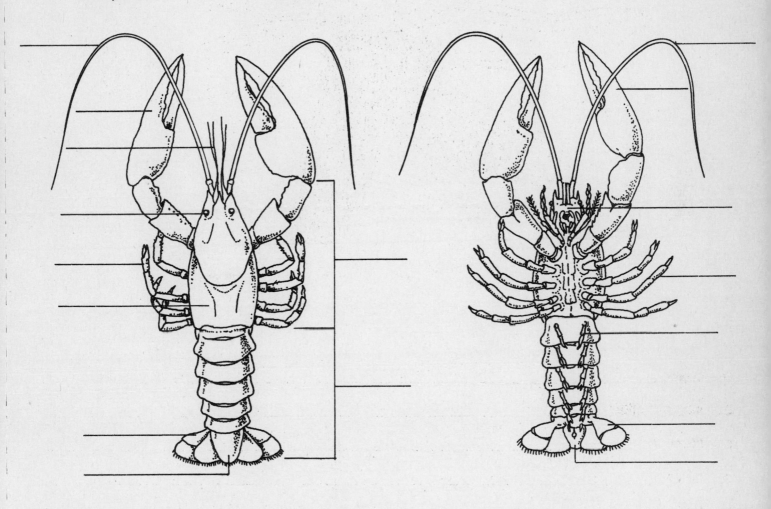

Fill in the blanks with the correct answers.

Crayfish seize their food with their _____. The _____ and

_____ crush and chew the food. The _____ are the

excretory organs. The _____ are used for respiration. The "brain" consists of

a pair of _____ . Two large nerves extend from the _____,

around the esophagus and join the _____ nerve cord.

STRUCTURE OF A BONY FISH

Name _____

Label the following parts of a fish on the diagrams below of the external and/or internal structure.

a. gills
b. brain
c. spinal cord
d. swimbladder
e. dorsal fins
f. caudal fin
g. anal fin

h. lateral line
i. operculum
j. gill filaments
k. mouth
l. intestine
m. pelvic fin
n. liver

o. stomach
p. heart
q. kidney
r. gall bladder
s. urinary bladder
t. urogenital opening

u. anus
v. ovary/testis
w. pyloric caeca
x. pectoral fin
y. eyes

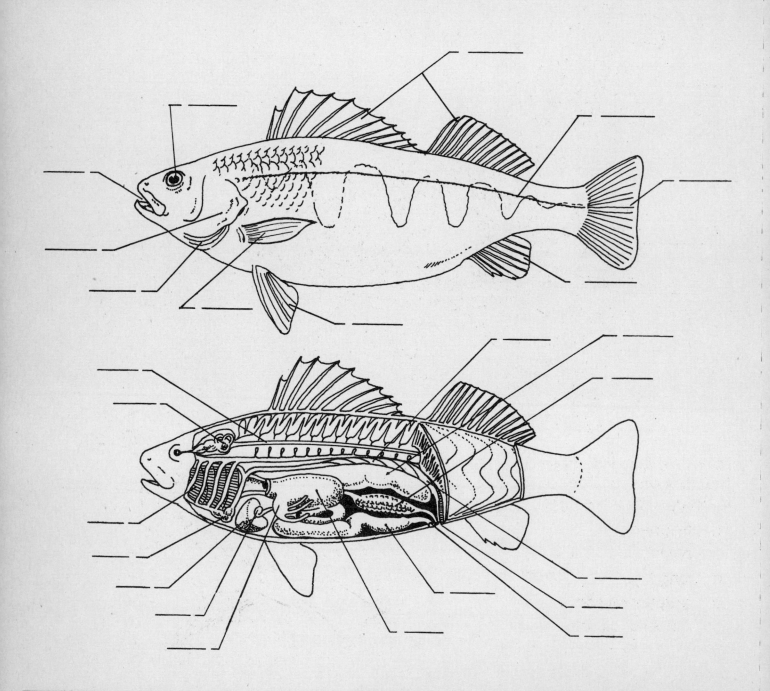

INTERNAL STRUCTURE OF A BIRD

Name _____

Label the following parts of the internal structure of a bird on the diagram below.

a. ureter   f. trachea   k. gall bladder
b. crop   g. kidney   l. gizzard
c. heart   h. cloaca
d. liver   i. esophagus
e. lung   j. intestine

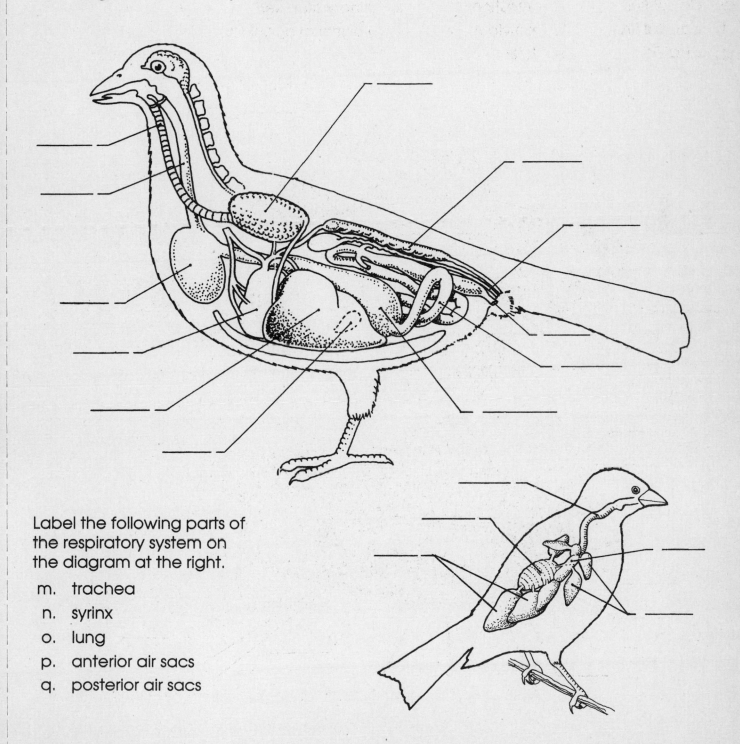

Label the following parts of the respiratory system on the diagram at the right.

m. trachea
n. syrinx
o. lung
p. anterior air sacs
q. posterior air sacs

THE HUMAN DIGESTIVE SYSTEM

Name _____

Label the following parts of the human digestive system on the diagram below.

a. mouth
b. salivary glands
c. esophagus
d. stomach
e. liver
f. pancreas
g. small intestine
h. large intestine
i. rectum
j. anus
k. appendix
l. gall bladder

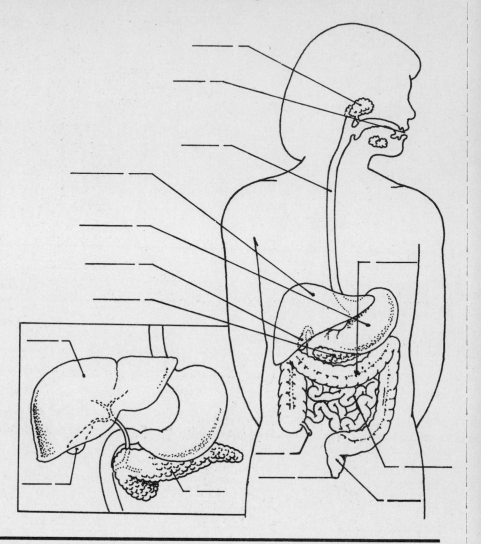

Accessory Organs

Food does not pass through three organs in the digestive system. Label the three accessory organs in the diagram to the right.

m. liver
n. gall bladder
o. pancreas

Fill in the blanks below with the correct answers.

Food passes from the _____ to the _____ to the _____ and then to the _____ , where gastric juices break up proteins and other molecules. From the stomach, food passes to the _____ , where nutrients are absorbed into the body's bloodstream. Undigested material moves into the _____ or colon, where water is resorbed and the residual materials is compacted. This material, now known as feces, moves into the _____ where it is stored temporarily until it passes out of the _____ . Above the stomach is the _____ , which plays many important roles in digestion, and nested below the stomach is the _____ , which secretes many of the digestive enzymes.

THE MOUTH AND TEETH

Name _____

Label the following parts of the tooth on the diagram below.

a. gum
b. nerves and blood vessels
c. dentin
d. enamel
e. pulp
f. crown
g. neck
h. root
i. cementum
j. bone

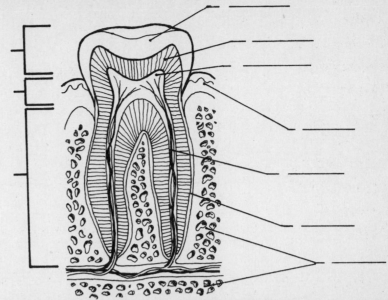

Teeth in Your Jaw

The diagram shows the teeth in your upper jaw. Label the four kinds of teeth. Then, indicate what kind of tooth is used for: cutting food, tearing and shredding food; grinding and crushing food.

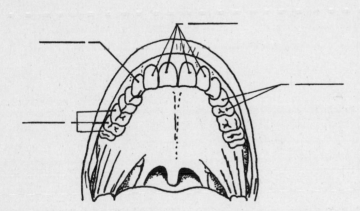

l. incisors _____
m. canines _____
n. premolars _____
o. molars _____

Salivary Glands

The mouth contains three pair of salivary glands. Label these glands in the diagram to the right.

p. parotid
q. submaxillary
r. sublingual

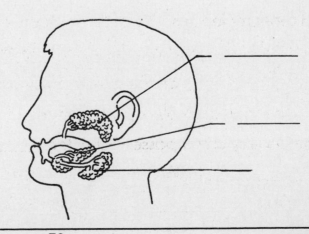

HUMAN DIGESTIVE SYSTEM CROSSWORD

Name _____

Across

5. Chemical digestion of carbohydrates begins here.

6. Enzyme that begins the digestion of proteins

8. Produced by the liver, this emulsifies fats to make digestion easier.

10. Acid present in the stomach

11. Tube between the mouth and stomach

12. Water and certain vitamins are absorbed here from the undigested food.

Down

1. Wastes are stored here before expulsion

2. Fingerlike projections which increase the surface area of the small intestine

3. Long, convoluted tube where chemical digestion is completed

4. Enzyme present in saliva

7. Involuntary muscle contraction that move the food through the digestive system

9. In this muscular pouch, food is mixed with gastric juice.

STRUCTURE OF THE HEART

Name _____

Label the following parts of the human heart on the diagram below.

a. aorta
b. left pulmonary artery
c. left pulmonary vein
d. left atrium
e. bicuspid valve (mitral valve)
f. left ventricle
g. septum
h. right ventricle
i. inferior vena cava
j. semilunar valves
k. tricuspid valve
l. right atrium
m. right pulmonary vein
n. right pulmonary artery
o. superior vena cava

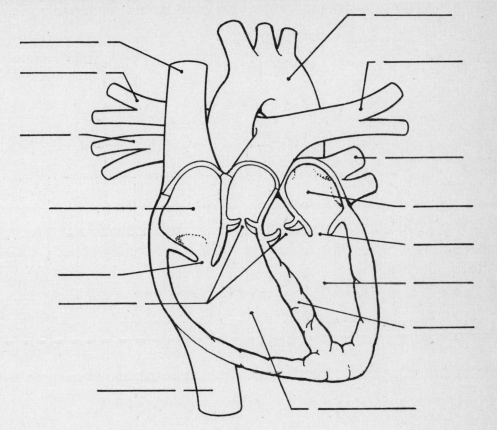

Heartbeat

Fill in the blanks with the correct answers.
Then, label the nodes in the diagram to the right.

The heart beats regularly because it has its own

pacemaker. The pacemaker is a small region of

muscle called the sinoatrial, or SA, node. It is in the

upper back wall of the right _____.

The _____ node triggers an impulse

that causes both atria to _____.

Very quickly, the impulse reaches the

atrioventricular, or AV, node at the bottom of the

_____ atrium. Immediately, the

_____ node triggers an impulse that

causes both _____ to contract.

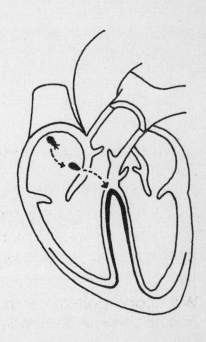

HUMAN CIRCULATORY SYSTEM

Name _____

Starting from and ending with the right atrium, trace the flow of blood through the heart and body by numbering the following in the correct order.

_____ right atrium   _____ lungs

_____ left atrium   _____ right ventricle

_____ pulmonary artery   _____ left ventricle

_____ vena cava   _____ body cells

_____ aorta   _____ pulmonary veins

Starting from and ending with the heart, trace the blood flow through the human circulatory system by numbering the following in the correct order.

_____ heart   _____ capillaries

_____ veins   _____ arteries

_____ arterioles   _____ venules

What term best fits each of the following descriptions?

1. vessels which carry blood away from the heart _____

2. vessels which carry blood toward the heart _____

3. tiny blood vessels with walls that are only one cell thick _____

4. thick wall that divides the heart into two sides _____

5. upper chambers of the heart that receive blood _____

6. lower chambers of the heart that pump blood out of the heart _____

7. valve between right atrium and right ventricle _____

8. valve between left atrium and left ventricle _____

9. valves found between the ventricles and blood vessels _____

10. membrane around the heart _____

11. the only artery in the body rich in carbon dioxide _____

12. the only vein in the body rich in oxygen _____

THE BLOOD

Label the following parts on the diagram at the right.
   a. white blood cell
   b. red blood cell
   c. platelet

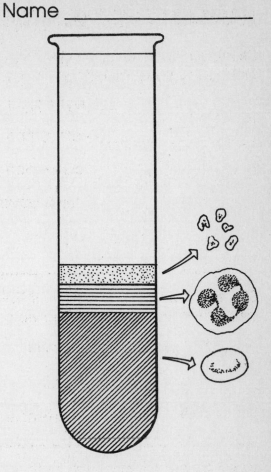

Answer the questions below.

   1. What is the role of platelets? _____

   _____

   _____

   2. What are sickle cells? _____

   _____

   _____

   3. Why are they important? _____

   _____

   _____

Match the description In Column I with the correct term in Column II.

Column I	Column II
a. iron-containing molecule in red blood cells	_____ plasma
b. white blood cells which produce antibodies	_____ platelets
c. liquid part of the blood	_____ lymphocytes
d. returns tissue fluid to the blood	_____ antigens
e. cell fragments involved in clotting	_____ fibrin
f. foreign molecules in the body	_____ hemoglobin
g. cancer of the bone marrow	_____ antibodies
h. condition in which the blood cannot carry sufficient oxygen	_____ anemia
i. strands of protein involved in clotting	_____ leukemia
j. react with antigens and inactivates them	_____ lymphatic system

BLOOD TYPES AND TRANSFUSIONS

Name _____

Fill in the blanks on the table below. Then answer the questions.

Blood Type	Antigens on Red Cells	Antibodies in Plasma	May Donate To	May Receive From
A				
B				
AB				
O				

1. Why are individuals with blood type O considered universal donors? _____

   _____

2. Why are individuals with blood type AB considered universal recipients? _____

   _____

3. Today, some people who know they must undergo surgery in the near future give their own blood at the blood bank earlier. Then, they use it during surgery. Why?

   _____

The distribution of blood types around the world varies. For example, you would find it different in Japan, and among Basque people in northern Spain.

POPULATION	A	B	AB	O
U.S. Whites	39.7%	10.6%	3.4%	46.3%
U.S. Blacks	26.5%	20.1%	4.3%	49.1%
Native Americans	30.6%	0.2%	0.00%	69.1%

On the basis of the table, answer the following questions.

1. In the U.S., what is the most frequent blood type? _____

2. If you are an African American, what are the chances that your blood is type A?

   _____

3. What is the only population that has no representative with one blood type?

   _____

4. What blood type is this? _____

5. Compare the frequency of type B blood between white and black Americans.

   _____

THE HUMAN RESPIRATORY SYSTEM

Respiratory System

Label the following parts of the human respiratory system on the diagram.

a. nasal passage   h. bronchiole
b. nostrils   i. alveoli
c. mouth   j. diaphragm
d. epiglottis   k. lung
e. larynx   l. pharynx
f. trachea   m. pleura
g. bronchi

Gas Exchange

The table shows what happens to the air we inhale.

Gas	Inhaled	Exhaled
oxygen (O_2)	20.71%	14.6%
carbon dioxide (CO_2)	0.04%	4.0%
water (H_2O)	1.25%	5.9%

1. What gas is removed from inhaled air? _____

2. What gases are added to inhaled air and then exhaled? _____ and _____

3. Which gas shows the greatest difference in percent between inhaled and exhaled air? _____

Fill in the blanks below with the correct answers.

Inspired air rich in _____ enters the body through the _____

or _____. It passes through the _____ and

_____, or voice box, and into the _____. Air then enters

each _____, which branches into _____, and finally into the

air sacs or _____ of the _____. The lungs are housed in the

_____ cavity that is bound on the bottom by a thin layer of muscle, the

_____. Each lung is covered by a very thin _____

membrane. In the alveoli, _____ is exchanged for oxygen.

HUMAN RESPIRATORY SYSTEM CROSSWORD

Name _____

Across

3. Area at the back of the throat where the mouth and nasal cavity meet
4. The trachea divides into these right and left branches
5. Opening to the windpipe
7. Contains the vocal cords
10. Tiny air sacs where the exchange of gases between air and blood takes place
11. Flat sheet of muscle separating the chest cavity from the abdominal cavity
14. Inflammation of the lining of the bronchial tubes

Down

1. Smaller branches of the bronchi
2. Flap of tissue which prevents food from entering windpipe during swallowing
6. Tube leading from larynx to bronchi
8. blood vessels surrounding the air sacs
9. Moist membrane covering the lung and chest cavity wall on each side
12. Infection of the lungs caused by viruses, bacteria or fungi
13. Bronchial spasm resulting in decreased air movement and air trapped in alveoli

HUMAN SKIN

Label the following parts of human skin on the diagram below.

a. pore
b. hair
c. nerve ending
d. fat cells
e. capillary
f. sweat gland
g. hair follicle
h. epidermis
i. dermis
j. erector muscle
k. subcutaneous tissue

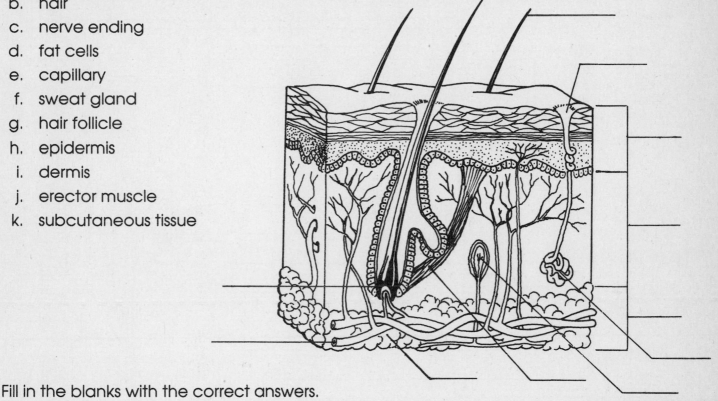

Fill in the blanks with the correct answers.

_____ makes up the skin of the body and the lining of the respiratory and

digestive tracts. _____ is the largest organ of the vertebrate body,

composing 15% of the actual weight in an adult. Vertebrate skin is composed of two

layers: the outer _____ and the lower _____. There is a

protective underlying layer, or _____ layer. Cells are constantly lost from

the _____ and replaced by new cells produced deep within the

epidermis. It takes about 27 days for all of the outer skin cells to be _____.

Specialized cells called melanocytes within the epidermis produce a brownish pigment

called _____ . People of all races have about the same number of

melanocytes but differ in the amount of _____ produced, thus giving a

vast range of skin tones. The dermis is composed mainly of _____ tissue,

which gives the skin its strength and elasticity. Among the structures in the dermis are

blood _____, nerves, hair _____, oil _____

and _____ glands. Wrinkling of the skin occurs in the _____

layer. Leather goods are made of animal _____.

HUMAN URINARY TRACT AND KIDNEY

Name _____

Label the parts of the human urinary system, including the human kidney, in the diagram below. Give the function/purpose of each part.

a. kidneys _____

b. adrenal glands _____

c. ureter _____

_____

d. urinary bladder_____

_____

e. urethra _____

_____

f. renal artery _____

_____

g. renal vein _____

_____

h. cortex _____

_____

i. medulla_____

_____

j. renal pelvis_____

_____

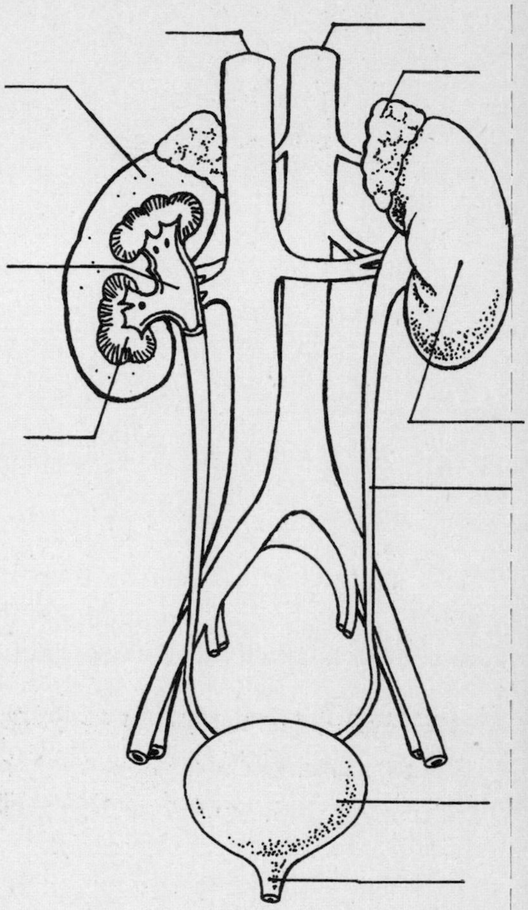

Fill in the blanks below with the correct answers.

Kidneys are the "filters" of the _____ system. They control essential

balance between body salts and _____. They remove from the blood

nitrogenous wastes, water, urea, nonvolatile foreign substances, excess salt and excess

water. The kidney is enclosed by a connective tissue _____and is divided

into an outer _____ and an inner _____. The

_____ functions chiefly for water resorption. The liquid waste,

_____, collected by the kidneys passes through the _____

to the _____. The urinary bladder is a strong muscular organ that stores the

urine until it can be excreted via the _____.

THE NEPHRON

Structure of Nephron

Label the parts of a nephron on the diagram to the right.

a. Bowman's capsule
b. renal arteriole
c. glomerulus
d. capillaries
e. loop of Henle
f. collecting tubule

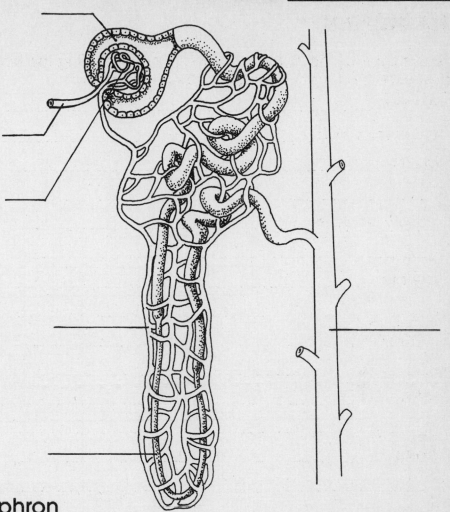

Functioning of the Nephron

The diagram indicates that the nephrons remove wastes from the blood by the process of filtration and reabsorption. Filtration takes place in the glomerulus; reabsorption takes place in the loop of Henle.

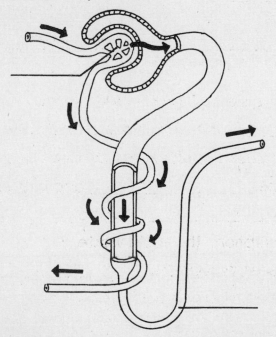

Label these two parts. Indicate the areas where filtration and reabsorption take place. Tell whether each of the following substances that is filtered from the blood in the glomerulus is reabsorbed, excreted as part of the urine, or both.

water _____

amino acids _____

glucose _____

salt _____

urea _____

HUMAN EXCRETORY SYSTEM CROSSWORD

Name _____

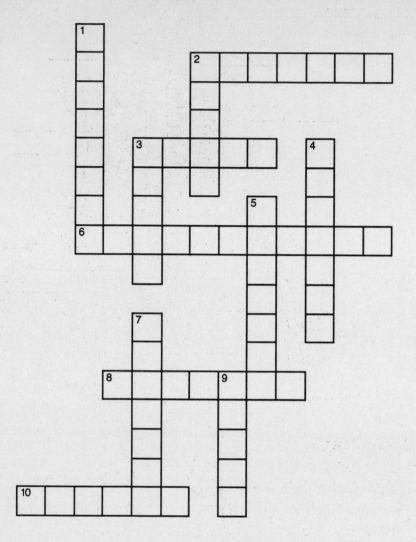

Across

2. Tubes connecting the kidneys to the urinary bladder

3. Carbon dioxide and water are excreted here during exhalation

6. Structures in the skin which excrete water, salts and some urea

8. Urine is expelled from the body through this tube

10. Arteries and veins to kidneys

Down

1. Microscopic units that filter the blood in the kidneys

2. Lquid waste collected and excreted by the kidneys

3. Removes toxic substances from the blood and converts excess amino acids to urea

4. Organs that filter wastes and other dissolved substances out of the blood

5. The urinary ____ stores the urine until it can be excreted by the body.

7. Endocrine gland at the top of each kidney

9. Loop of ____ at the bottom of nephron

THE HUMAN SKELETAL SYSTEM

Name _____

Label the following parts of the human skeletal system on the diagram.

a. skull
b. cranium
c. mandible
d. clavicle
e. pectoral girdle
f. scapula
g. sternum
h. ribs
i. humerus
j. vertebrae
k. vertebral column
l. pelvic girdle
m. radius
n. ulna
o. carpals
p. metacarpals
q. phalanges
(on both hands and feet)
r. femur
s. patella
t. tibia
u. fibula
v. tarsals
w. metatarsals

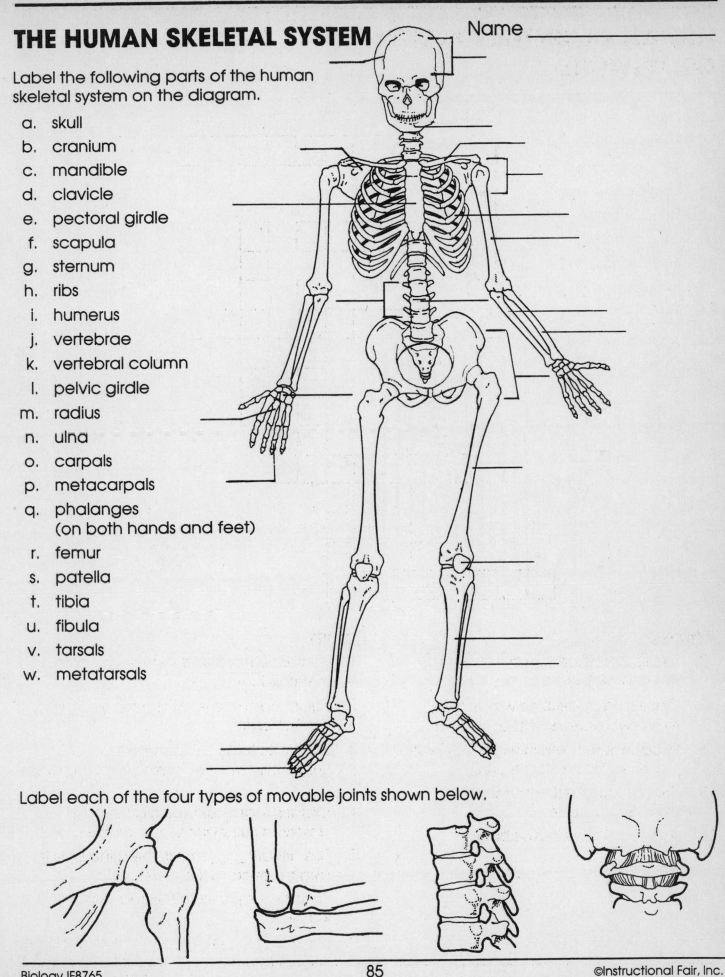

Label each of the four types of movable joints shown below.

STRUCTURE OF BONES

Name _____

Label the following parts of a long bone on both diagrams wherever possible. The diagram at the right shows a longitudinal section, the other a cross section.

a. shaft
b. periosteum
c. blood vessels
d. compact bone
e. spongy bone
f. red marrow
g. nerve cells
h. lamella

i. Haversian canal
j. bone cell

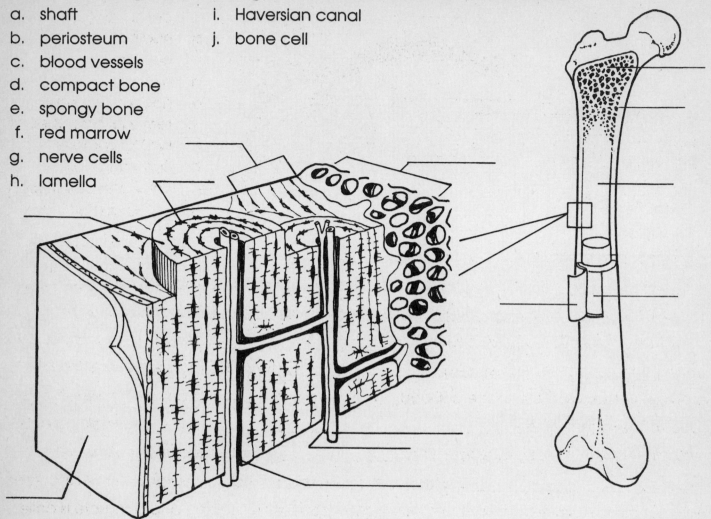

Fill in the blanks with the correct answers.

A bone is covered with a thin, tough membrane called the _____. It

supplies bone cells with _____ and _____ using its rich supply

of blood vessels. The dense part of bone is called _____ bone.

_____ is the mineral that gives bone its strength. The ends of bones are

made up of _____ bone, which has many spaces. These spaces are filled

with bone _____. Most bones contain yellow _____, which is

made up of nerve cells, blood vessels and fat cells. New blood cells are made in

_____ marrow. _____ connect bones. _____

connect muscles to bone.

NEURON AND NEUROMUSCULAR JUNCTION

Name _____

Neuron
Label the diagram at the left.

a. cell body (cyton)
b. nucleus
c. dendrites
d. axon
e. node of Ranvier
f. terminal branches
g. synaptic knobs
h. Schwann cell
i. Schwann cell nucleus
j. myelin sheath

Fill in the blanks with the correct answers.

_____ are specialized for the transmission of nerve impulses. The nucleus is located in the _____ of the neuron. From the cell body, two types of structures carry out transmission functions. _____ transmit nerve impulses from other cells or sensory systems. _____ provide for the transmission of nerve impulses away from the cell body. A single neuron cell can be over a meter long due to the length of its _____. _____ are the supporting cells associated with axons. They form a(an) _____ around many vertebrate neurons. _____ interrupt the myelin sheath were the axon is in direct contact with surrounding intercellular fluid. The junction between a neuron and a muscle is called a(an) _____ junction. _____ is the neurotransmitter. At a neuromuscular junction, acetylcholine released from a(an) _____ depolarizes the muscle cell membrane and triggers muscle contractions.

Neuromuscular Junction
Label the following parts of a neuromuscular junction.

a. axon
b. cleft
c. synaptic knob
d. muscle fiber
e. acetylcholine sacs

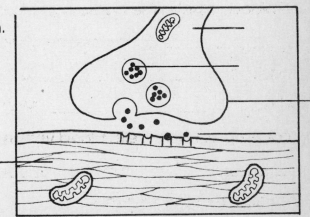

SPINAL CORD AND REFLEX ACT

Name _____

Cross Section of Spinal Cord

Label the following parts of a spinal cord on the cross-section diagram.

a. white matter
b. grey matter
c. dorsal root ganglion
d. nerve fibers
e. interneuron
f. synapse
g. sensory neuron
h. motor neuron

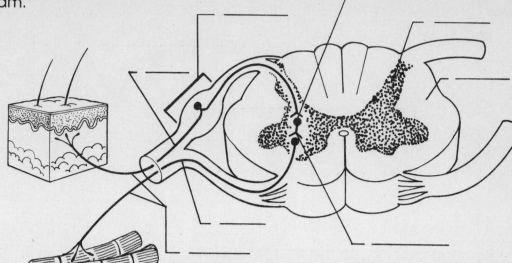

Reflex Act

Label the following parts of a reflex act on the diagram of a boy stepping on a tack and jerking his leg away.

a. sensory neuron
b. motor neuron
c. stimulus
d. spinal cord
e. receptor (in skin)
f. effector (muscle)

Fill in the blanks with the correct answers.

Suppose you stepped on a tack. You jerked your leg away _____ you were aware of what happened. The impulse traveled from the _____, the skin, along a(an) _____ neuron into the _____. The impulse jumped across a(an) _____ to a(an) _____; then across another synapse to a _____ neuron. The impulse traveled along this nerve to a muscle, _____, in your leg. You jerked your leg away. Only a fraction of a second later, a(an) _____ traveled up your _____ to your _____ . But you had _____ reacted. This kind of reaction is known as a(an) _____. Reflex acts occur without thinking.

STRUCTURE OF THE BRAIN

Name _____

Label the correct parts of the brain and spinal cord on the diagram at the left below. Give the purpose/function of each part.

a. cerebellum _____

b. medulla oblongata _____

c. thalamus _____

d. hypothalamus _____

e. corpus callosum _____

f. pons _____

g. spinal cord _____

h. cerebrum _____

i. pituitary gland _____

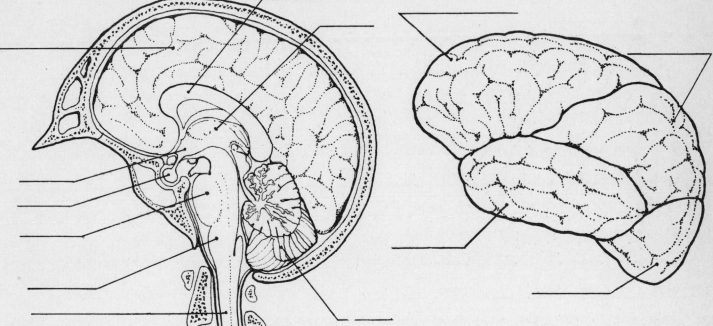

Lobes of the Cerebrum

The diagram to the right above shows the four major lobes of each hemisphere of the cerebrum: frontal, parietal, occipital and temporal. Label each lobe. Then, fill in the blanks below with the correct answers.

The _____ lobes control some body movements, reasoning, judgment and

emotions. The sense of vision is located in the _____ lobe. The sense of

hearing is interpreted in the _____ lobes. The _____ lobes

interpret sensations such as pain, pressure, touch, hot and cold.

STRUCTURE OF THE HUMAN EYE

Name _____

Label the parts of the human eye on the diagram below.

a. aqueous humor
b. cornea
c. pupil
d. lens
e. iris
f. ciliary body
g. vitreous humor
h. retina
i. optic nerve
j. choroid coat
k. sclera
l. suspensory ligament

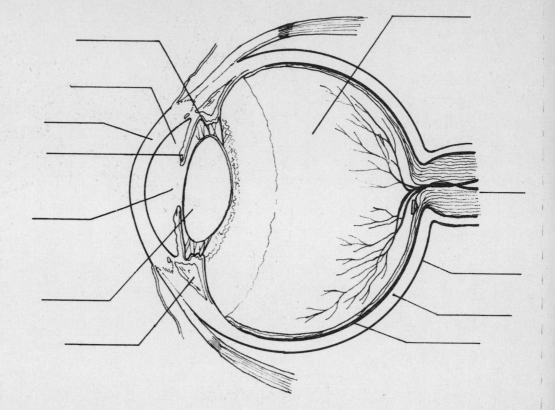

Fill in the blanks with the correct answers.

Light passes through a transparent layer, the _____ , which begins to focus the light onto the rear of the eye. Light then passes through the _____ , the major focusing structure. The lens is held in place by suspending ligaments to _____ . Contraction of these muscles changes the shape of the lens and thus the _____ . The _____ , located between the cornea and the lens, controls the amount of light entering the eye. The iris reduces the size of the transparent zone, or _____ of the eye. The _____ , in the back of the eye, contains about 3 million _____ which detect color and one billion _____ which detect light and dark. The central region of the retina where images are focused is called the _____ . The _____ transmits visual impulses directly to the brain. People whose point of focus lies in front of the fovea are said to be _____ . If the point of focus lies behind the fovea, they are called _____ . Corrective lenses may be used to focus the image onto the _____ , thus correcting the condition.

STRUCTURE OF THE HUMAN EAR

Name _____

Label the parts of the ear on the diagram below.

a. auditory canal
b. eardrum
c. hammer
d. anvil
e. semicircular canals
f. cochlea
g. auditory nerve
h. Eustachian tube
i. stirrup
j. earlobe
k. oval window

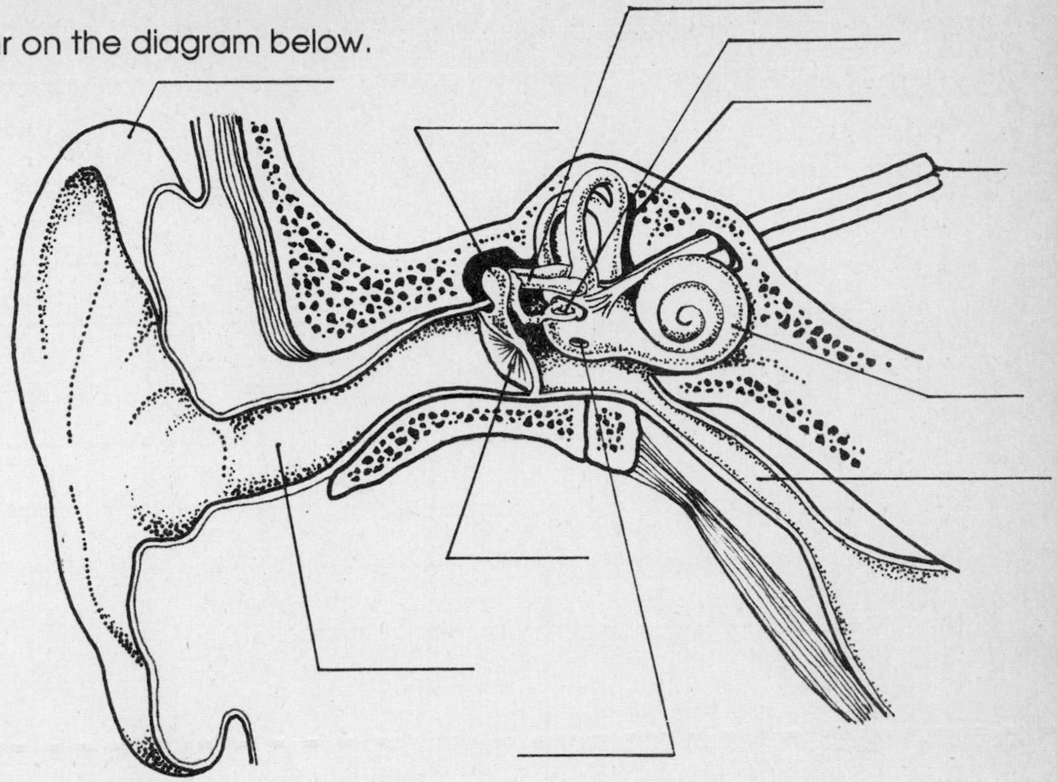

Fill In the blanks with the correct answers.

Sound waves beat against a large membrane of the outer ear called the eardrum or

_____. In the _____ these vibrations are transferred by the

three small bones, _____, _____ and _____,

which increase the force of the vibration. The _____ presses against the

_____ which is smaller than the tympanic membrane. The

_____ connects the throat to the middle ear and serve to equalize air

pressure. Hearing actually takes place on the other side of the oval window, in the

_____. The fluid-filled chamber of the inner ear is called the

_____. It accepts the wave motion that then travels through the vestibular

and tympanic canals. Where the sound waves beat against the sides of the canals,

_____ bend and _____ transmit impulses. The

_____ carries this information to the brain where it is interpreted.

The upper part of the inner ear contains three _____. These are positioned

at _____ angles to each other and are filled with _____. The

semicircular canals help to maintain _____.

NERVOUS SYSTEM CROSSWORD

Name _____

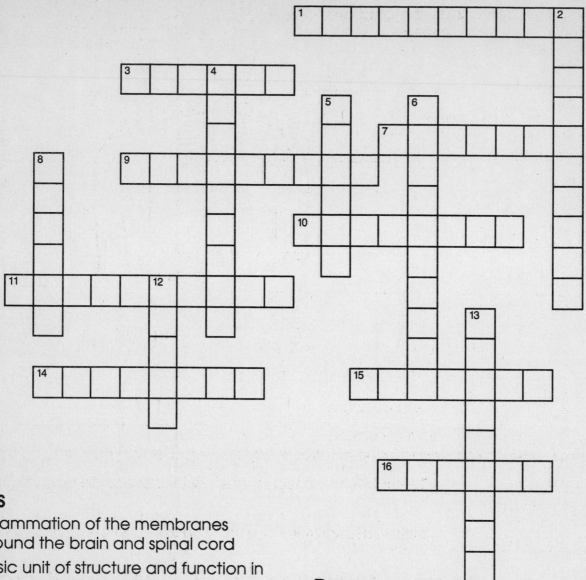

Across

1. Inflammation of the membranes around the brain and spinal cord
3. Basic unit of structure and function in the nervous system
7. Controls involuntary activities such as breathing and heartbeat
9. Muscles and glands, for example
10. Largest part of the brain; where thought occurs
11. All nerves that are not part of the central nervous system
14. Complex, unlearned, involuntary behavior
15. Nervous system that controls the voluntary skeletal muscles
16. Damage to the brain due to a hemorrhage or blood clot

Down

2. Nerve pathway between the brain and other parts of the body
4. Sense organs
5. Bundles of neurons that transmit impulses over long distances
6. Part of the brain that coordinates voluntary activities and balance
8. Inborn, involuntary response to a particular stimulus
12. Response repeated constantly until it becomes automatic
13. Nervous system that controls the activities of the internal organs

THE HUMAN ENDOCRINE SYSTEM

Name _____

Label the following parts on the diagram of the human endocrine system.

a. pineal

b. hypothalamus

c. pituitary

d. thyroid

e. parathyroids

f. thymus

g. adrenal

h. pancreas

i. ovary (female)

j. testis (male)

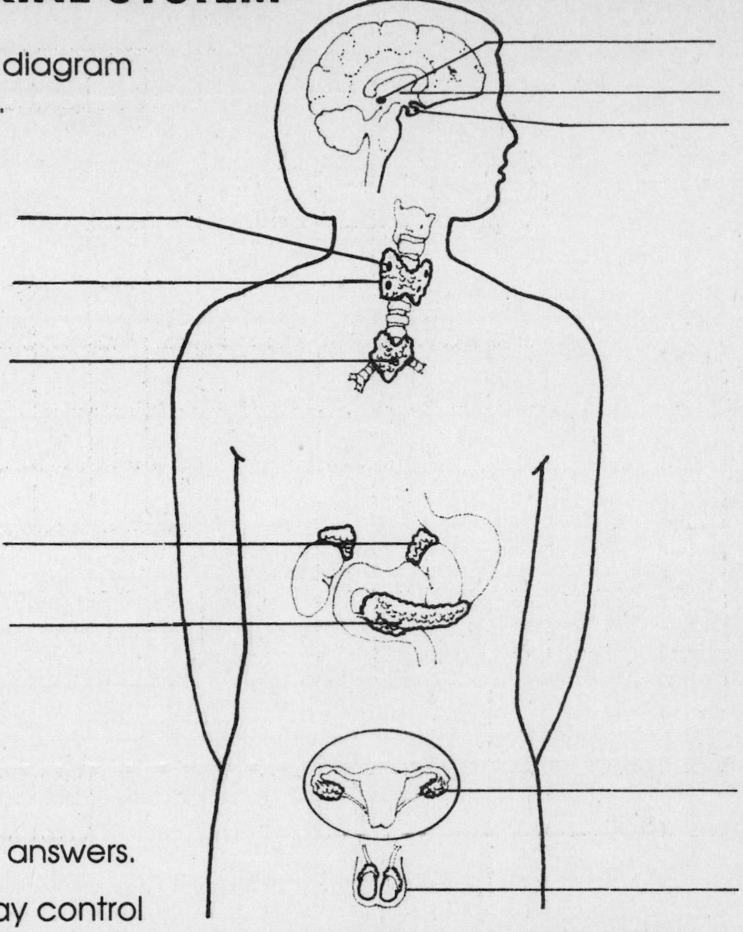

Fill in the blanks with the correct answers.

1. _____ gland may control biorhythms in some animals and control the onset of puberty in humans.

2. _____ gland stimulates metabolic rate and is essential to normal growth and development.

3. _____ gland stimulates growth and stimulates secretion of hormones from other glands.

4. _____ in females stimulates development of secondary sex characteristics, stimulates growth of sex organs at puberty, and prompts monthly preparation of uterus for pregnancy.

5. _____ is the major area where the nervous and endocrine systems interact.

6. _____ controls blood glucose levels and determines the fate of glycogen.

7. _____ gland initiates stress responses, increases heart rate, blood pressure, and metabolic rate, dilates blood vessels, mobilizes fat and raises blood sugar levels.

8. _____ gland promotes production and maturation of white blood cells.

9. _____ in males stimulates development of secondary sex characteristics, stimulates growth spurt at puberty, stimulates spermatogenesis.

10. _____ gland increases blood calcium level, stimulates calcium reabsorption and activates vitamin D.

HUMAN HORMONES

Name _____

Listed below are the major hormones produced by the human body.

ACTH	estrogen	Luteinizing hormone	testosterone
adrenaline	FSH	noradrenaline	thyroxin
aldosterone	glucagon	parathormone	TSH
calcitonin	growth hormone	prolactin	
cortisol	insulin	progesterone	

Next to each gland listed below, write the name of the hormone or hormones it produces.

1. pituitary _____

2. thyroid _____

3. parathyroid _____

4. adrenal _____

5. pancreas (islets of Langerhans) _____

6. testis _____

7. ovary _____

Next to each of the functions listed below, write the name of the hormone that produces this effect.

8. raises the blood sugar level and increases the
   heartbeat and breathing rates   _____

9. causes glucose to be removed from the blood
   and stored   _____

10. influences the development of female secondary
    sex characteristics   _____

11. promotes the conversion of glycogen to glucose   _____

12. controls the metabolism of calcium   _____

13. promotes the reabsorbation of sodium and potassium
    ions by the kidney   _____

14. influences the development of male secondary sex
    characteristics   _____

15. stimulates the elongation of the long bones of the body _____

16. stimulates the secretion of hormones by the cortex of
    the adrenal glands   _____

17. regulates the rate of metabolism in the body   _____

18. stimulates the development of eggs in the female's ovary _____

19. involved in the regulation of carbohydrate , protein
    and fat metabolism   _____

20. stimulates the production of thyroxin   _____

THE MALE REPRODUCTIVE SYSTEM

Label the parts of the male reproductive system on the diagram below.

a. urinary bladder
b. prostate gland
c. urethra
d. penis
e. vas deferens
f. scrotum
g. testis
h. Cowper's gland
i. seminal vesicle
j. epididymis

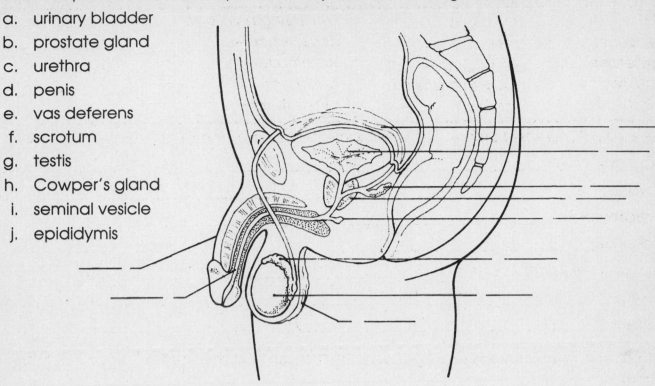

Fill in the blanks with the correct answers.

_____ occurs in the _____ producing sperm with 23 _____. Each human sperm cell has _____ parts—a head, a middle region and a _____. The head contains the _____ with the _____. The acrosome at the tip of the head enables the sperm to _____ the _____. The middle region contains the _____, which produce energy. The tail, a long and slender _____, moves the sperm.

The testes are housed in the _____. From the testes, sperm passes through the _____, which is a storage and maturation area, to the _____ where they are housed until delivery. The _____ at the base of the urethra secretes a fluid that has a stimulating effect on the sperm. During intercourse, they travel to the _____, where the reproductive and urinary tracts join, emptying through the _____. An adult male produces _____ continuously, several hundred million each day of his life. Those that are not ejaculated from the body are _____ in a continual cycle of renewal.

THE FEMALE REPRODUCTIVE SYSTEM

Name _____

Label the parts of the female reproductive system on the diagram.

a. ovary
b. uterus
c. urinary bladder
d. urethra
e. vagina
f. cervix
g. Fallopian tube

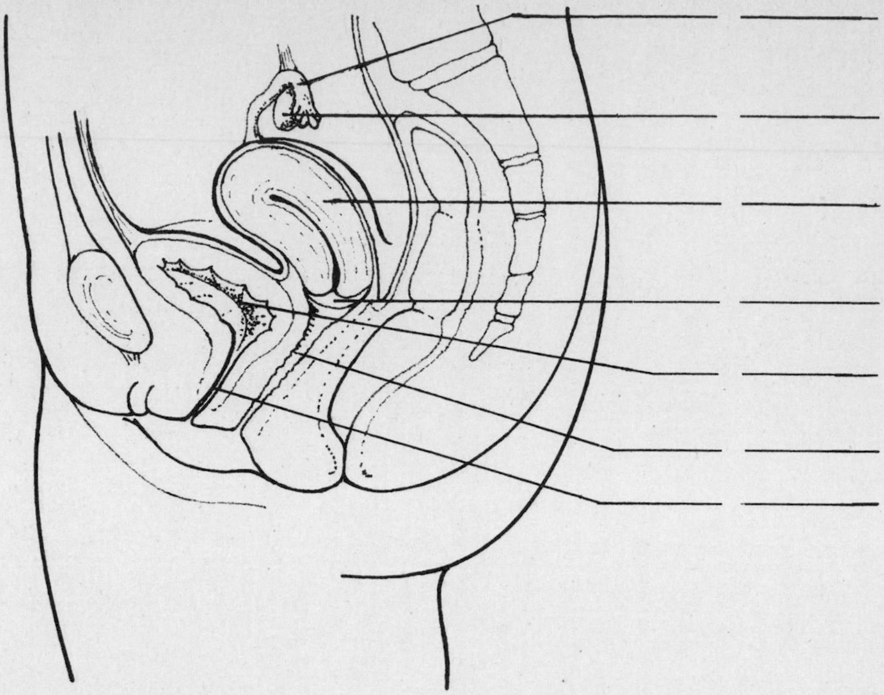

Fill in the blanks with the correct answers.

The female is born with about two million _____ halted at prophase I, only 400 of which will mature into _____ within her lifetime. On about the _____ day of the menstrual cycle, the ovum is released from a _____ on the surface of the _____ at ovulation. _____ move it into the _____. Sperm are deposited in the _____ which leads to the mouth of the _____. They must make their way through the _____, the muscular sphincter at the opening of the uterus, through the uterus, and up the Fallopian tube to fertilize the ovum within about 24 hours or the ovum will die. Peristaltic contractions move the ovum or zygote to the _____ in about three days. If the ovum is not fertilized and implanted, _____ will occur on day 28.

In any egg cell, the sex chromosome is a (an) _____ chromosome. In a sperm cell, the sex chromosome is either a (an) _____ or a (an) _____ chromosome. If a sperm with an X chromosome fertilized the egg, the sex chromosome pattern of the fertilized egg is _____ and the offspring will be a _____. If a sperm with a Y chromosome fertilizes the egg, the sex chromosome pattern of the fertilized egg is _____ and the offspring will be a _____.

A MAMMAL EMBRYO

Name _____

Label the parts of the embryo in utero in the diagram below. Give the function/purpose of each part.

a. embryo _____

b. placenta _____

c. Fallopian tube _____

d. uterine wall _____

e. umbilical cord_____

_____

_____

f. amnion _____

_____

_____

g. amniotic fluid _____

_____

h. vagina_____

_____

_____

I. uterus_____

_____

_____

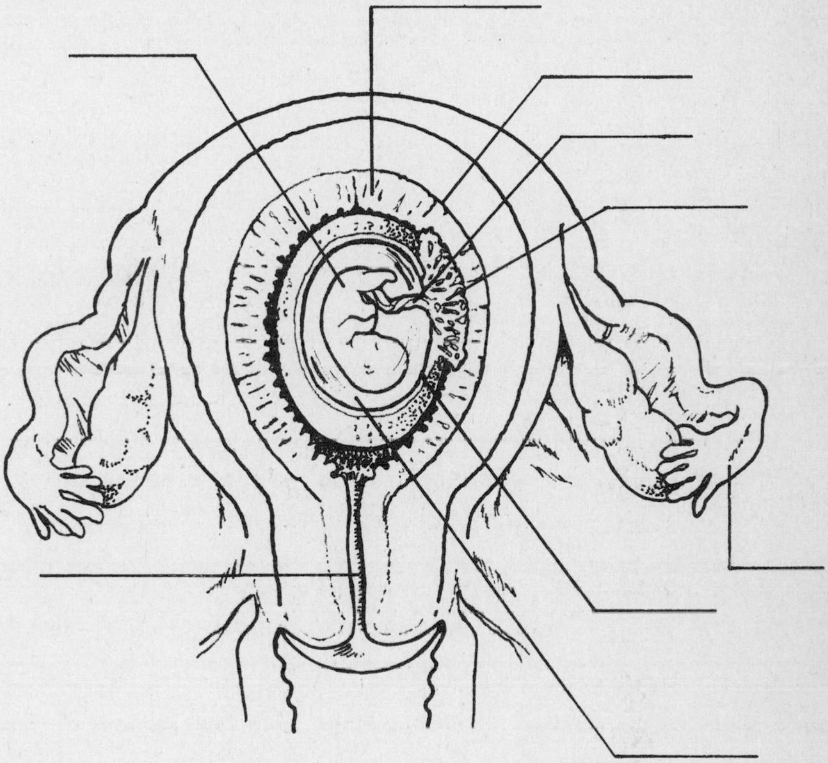

Fill in the blanks with the correct answers.

After two months of development, the embryo is called a (an) _____. The

_____ is formed in part from the inner lining of the uterus and in part from

other membranes. It is through the placenta that the embryo/fetus is nourished while in

the _____ and _____ are carried away. The

_____ connects the embryo/fetus with the placenta. It provides a transport

system for placental-fetal circulation. The _____ is the innermost of the

extra embryonic membranes, and it forms a fluid-filled _____, around the

embryo/fetus.

97   ©Instructional Fair, Inc.

HUMAN REPRODUCTION

Name _____

Fill in the blanks from the word list below. Words may be used more than once.

corpus luteum	implantation	ova	seminal fluid
estrogen	LH (luteinizing	progesterone	seminal vesicles
Fallopian tube	hormone)	prostate	testes
follicles	menstruation	puberty	uterus
FSH (follicle stimulating	ovary	scrotum	vagina
hormone)	ovulation	semen	vas deferens

The production of sperm takes place in the _____ . These paired glands are contained in a sac called the _____ . The sperm travel to the urethra through a long tube called the _____ . During this passage, _____ , secreted by the _____ , _____ and Cowper's glands are mixed with the sperm. This mixture is called _____ . During sexual intercourse, _____ is released through the urethra and deposited in the female's _____ .

The female gonad is called the _____ . A female is born with all the egg cells, or _____ , that she will ever have, but they are immature. Beginning at _____ , the hormone _____ is released from the pituitary to stimulate maturation of eggs. The eggs are contained in saclike structures called _____ . Usually, only one of the eggs matures fully each month. As the _____ enlarge, they secrete the hormone _____ , which causes the lining of the _____ to thicken. After about 9 to 19 days, a surge of the hormone _____ is released from the pituitary. This causes the fully developed _____ to rupture, releasing a mature egg. This is called _____ . The empty follicle now becomes a mass of yellow tissue called the _____ . This secretes the hormone _____ which further thickens the lining of the uterus in preparation for receiving and nourishing a fertilized egg. When the ovum is released during _____ , it enters a _____ and begins its journey to the uterus. If it encounters sperm during this journey, it may be fertilized and begin dividing. When the fertilized egg reaches the uterus, if all goes well, _____ will occur and a pregnancy will be established. If no fertilization occurs, the _____ disintegrates in 13–15 days and _____ occurs. Then the cycle begins again.

HUMAN ENDOCRINE AND REPRODUCTION CROSSWORD

Across

1. Endocrine gland at base of brain
4. Hormone that causes follicle to mature
6. At the base of brain, gland that interacts with pituitary
7. Hormone produced by thyroid
9. Pituitary hormone that targets adrenal cortex
11. Organ through which sperm leaves the body
13. Tube leading from uterus to outside of body
14. Sac containing testes
17. Tube joining ovary to uterus
18. Houses developing embryo
19. Fluid-filled membrane surrounding embryo

Down

1. Gland that secretes insulin
2. Gland that secretes thyroxin
3. Organs that produce egg cells
5. Male reproductive glands
8. Hormone produced by adrenal medulla
10. Uterine membrane transports substances between mother and embryo
11. A gland that secretes seminal fluid
12. Ductless gland under breastbone
15. Neck of uterus
16. Hormone stimulates follicle production

TYPES OF DISEASES

Name _____

Diseases may be classified into several types; among these are inherited diseases, deficiency diseases, infectious diseases and hormonal diseases. First, indicate the type of disease. Then, identify the specific cause of each disease as deficiency, infectious, or hormonal. For inherited diseases, indicate whether it is sex-linked or the result of a defective gene or chromosome.

Disease	Type of Disease	Specific Cause
1. tetanus	_____	_____
2. diabetes	_____	_____
3. hemophilia	_____	_____
4. common cold	_____	_____
5. sickle-cell anemia	_____	_____
6. measles	_____	_____
7. Addison's disease	_____	_____
8. anemia	_____	_____
9. Down syndrome	_____	_____
10. AIDS	_____	_____
11. night blindness	_____	_____
12. tuberculosis	_____	_____
13. polio	_____	_____
14. Kleinfelter syndrome	_____	_____
15. colorblindness	_____	_____
16. pellagra	_____	_____
17. goiter	_____	_____
18. diptheria	_____	_____
19. rickets	_____	_____
20. pertussis	_____	_____

EVOLUTION

Name _____

Evidence of Evolution

Five evidences of evolution are (A) fossil evidence, (B) homologous structures, (C) embryology, (D) vestigial organs and (E) biochemical. Write the letter of the type of evidence by each example.

_____ 1. Bones in bird's wing and a human's arm are similar in structure.

_____ 2. All organisms use ATP in energy transfers.

_____ 3. There are similarities in structure among the early stages of fish, birds and humans.

_____ 4. Humans, unlike rabbits, have no known use for their appendix.

_____ 5. Horses have increased in size and decreased in number of toes since the Eocene.

Match the terms in Column I with the correct definition or name in Column II.

Column I

_____ 1. genetic drift

_____ 2. gradualism

_____ 3. Natural Selection

_____ 4. divergent evolution

_____ 5. punctuated equilibrium

_____ 6. mass extinction

_____ 7. mutations

_____ 8. gene pool

_____ 9. convergent evolution

_____ 10. radioactive dating

_____ 11. Use and Disuse

Column II

a. all genes in a population

b. brief periods of change interrupt long stable periods

c. changes in gene frequency in small populations

d. changes occur gradually over time

e. Darwin

f. determining age of fossils

g. gene or chromosomal changes

h. Lamarck

i. many species vanish at one time

j. Mendel

k. unrelated species become less alike

l. unrelated species become more alike

Darwin's Theory of Evolution

Number the steps of Darwin's theory in order.

_____ Struggle for Existence

_____ Overproduction

_____ Natural Selection

_____ Variation

ECOLOGICAL RELATIONSHIPS

Name _____

Food Webs

Use the food web below to answer questions 1-5.

1. When the hawk is the third-order consumer, the number of second-order consumers is

   _____ .

2. The food chain that includes insect-eating birds is ____

   _____ .

3. The animal that consumes the largest number of different types of first-order and second-order consumers is the

   _____ .

4. All the animals that are herbivores are

   _____ consumers.

5. If there were no snakes in this food web, the squirrels and rabbits could still be eaten by the _____ .

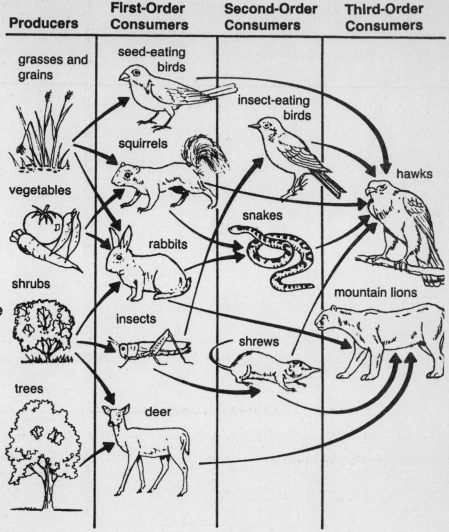

| | Producers | First-Order Consumers | Second-Order Consumers | Third-Order Consumers |

grasses and grains
seed-eating birds
squirrels
vegetables
insect-eating birds
rabbits
shrubs
snakes
insects
shrews
trees
deer
hawks
mountain lions

Ecological Terms

Fill in the blanks with the words from the list below.

| community | decomposers | ecosystem | habitat |
| herbivore | niche | omnivore | population | scavenger |

6. A group of independent organisms in a particular environment is a(an) _____ .

7. Organisms that break down complex compounds and dead tissue are _____ .

8. All the living and nonliving things in a selected area form a(an) _____ .

9. The particular environment to which a particular species is adapted is its _____ .

10. The special role and place of an organism within its habitat is its _____ .

11. An animal that eats both plants and animals is a(an) _____ .

12. Members of a single species that occupy a common area form a(an) _____ .

13. Animals that feed only on dead organisms are _____ .

ANSWER KEY

LABORATORY EQUIPMENT

Name _____

Label the following pieces of laboratory equipment.

a. Bunsen burner   d. tongs   g. beaker
b. balance   e. ring stand   h. graduated cylinder
c. funnel   f. Erlenmeyer flask   i. test tube
    j. test tube clamp

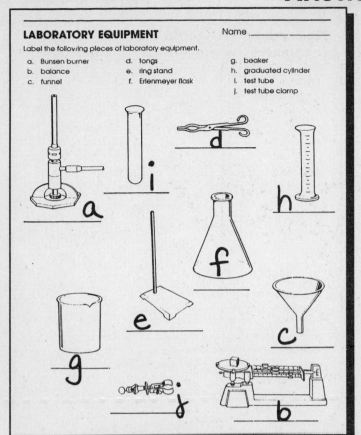

a, i, d, h, f, e, c, g, j, b

Page 1

THE SCIENTIFIC METHOD

Name _____

Put the following steps of the scientific method in the proper order.

6 Organize and analyze data
3 State a hypothesis
1 Identify the problem
7 State conclusion
4 Design and carry out an experiment
5 Make observations and record data
2 Gather information

Match the term in Column I with its definition in Column II.

Column I

1. theory f
2. law g
3. hypothesis a
4. experiment b
5. variable c
6. control e
7. data d
8. conclusion i
9. application h

Column II

a. suggested explanation to a problem or observation based upon known information

b. used to test a hypothesis

c. anything that can affect the results of an experiment

d. observations and measurements made during an experiment

e. part within the experiment that is maintained without change in order to provide a comparison for the part of the experiment containing the variable

f. hypothesis that has been tested and supported by a great amount of evidence over a long period of time

g. statement describing (but not explaining) a natural event or phenomenon

h. new use to which results are put or new technique developed

i. a summary that explains whether or not the data support the hypothesis

Page 2

THE SYSTEME INTERNATIONAL D'UNITES (SI)

Name _____

The measuring system used in science is the SI, which was adopted according to an international agreement reached in 1960. It is based on the metric system. The standard units in SI are:

Property	Unit	Symbol
mass	kilogram	kg
distance	meter	m
time	second	s
electric current	Ampere	A
temperature	Kelvin	K
amount of substance	mole	mol

As with the metric system, the SI utilizes prefixes to change the value of units. The following units are frequently used in science:

Prefix	Symbol	Value
mega-	M	1 000 000
kilo-	k	1 000
deci-	d	0.1
centi-	c	0.01
milli-	m	0.001
micro-	µ	0.000 001
nano-	n	0.000 000 0001

Example:
How many meters are equivalent to 500 mm?

$$500 \text{ mm} \times \frac{1m}{1\ 000\ mm} = 0.5 \text{ m}$$

Make the following conversions within the SI.

1. 3.0 m = **300** cm
2. 1,500 mL = **1.5** L
3. 35 cg = **0.35** g
4. 0.05 m = **50** mm
5. 2.5 L = **2500** mL
6. 0.25 km = **250** m
7. 50,000 µm = **0.05** m
8. 0.015 g = **15** mg
9. 75 cL = **0.75** L
10. 2,750 mg = **2.75** g

What would be a reasonable unit to use to measure the following?

11. distance from earth to moon **km**
12. length of a bacterium **µm**
13. mass of a bowling ball **kg**
14. mass of an aspirin tablet **mg**
15. dropperful of medicine **mL**

Page 3

SELF QUIZ—SCIENTIFIC METHOD AND THE SI SYSTEM

Name _____

Circle the letter of the correct answer.

1. In an experiment, one ___ is tested at a time to determine how it affects results.
   a. control   **b. variable**   c. problem   d. observation

2. The ___ describes the use of equipment and materials in an experiment.
   a. procedure   b. conclusion   c. control   d. problem

3. A ___ is the part of an experiment that provides a reliable standard for comparison
   a. procedure   b. theory   c. variable   **d. control**

4. The information already recorded about a scientific subject is the scientific ___.
   a. record   b. method   c. technique   d. experiment

5. ___ are the recorded facts and measurements from an experiment.
   a. Procedures   **b. Data**   c. Theories   d. inferences

6. The practical use of scientific knowledge is called ___.
   a. research   b. inferring   c. procedure   **d. technology**

7. A ___ is an explanation of observations that have been tested many times.
   a. conclusion   b. hypothesis   **c. theory**   d. record

8. A(n) ___ is a suggested solution to a scientific problem.
   a. observation   **b. hypothesis**   c. problem   d. procedure

9. Instruments and our senses are used to make ___ during an experiment.
   a. observations   b. hypotheses   c. problems   d. controls

10. A(n) ___ is performed under carefully controlled conditions to test a hypothesis.
    a. activity   b. observation   c. inference   **d. experiment**

11. A scientific ___ describes how nature words.
    a. record   **b. law**   c. hypothesis   d. result

12. To be accepted, a scientific discovery must produce ___ each time it is tested.
    a. the same results   b. the same hypothesis   c. new conclusions   d. new data

13. If after numerous tests a major hypothesis cannot be shown to be false, it may be accepted as ___.
    a. a control   **b. a theory**   c. data   d. an observation

14. New observations that do not agree with an accepted theory may cause the theory to be ___.
    a. explained   **b. rejected**   c. proven   d. recognized

Page 4

ANSWER KEY

SELF QUIZ . . . CONTINUED   Name _____

15. A ___ is a logical explanation to a problem based on observation.
    a. control   b. theory   (c.) conclusion   d. procedure
16. The commonly used unit in the measurement of temperature in the Biology laboratory is the ___.
    a. Kelvin   b. Celsius   (c.) Fahrenheit   d. boiling point
17. The ___ is the unit of time in the SI system.
    a. day   (b.) second   c. minute   d. hour
18. A ___ is a fixed quantity used for comparison.
    a. procedure   b. variable   (c.) standard   d. prefix
19. The unit of mass commonly used in the laboratory is the ___ .
    a. meter   b. cubic meter   (c.) gram   d. kilometer
20. The space occupied by an object is its ___ .
    (a.) volume   b. height   c. width   d. length
21. The amount of matter in an object is its ___ .
    (a.) mass   b. volume   c. size   d. balance
22. A scale commonly used by scientists for measuring temperature is the ___ scale.
    a. degree   (b.) Celsius   c. boiling point   d. Fahrenheit
23. There are ___ in one kilogram.
    a. 0.001 grams   b. 1000 milligrams   c. 0.001 milligrams   (d.) 1000 grams
24. Standards are important for comparing observations and are used ___ .
    (a.) by everyone   c. only for counting things
    b. only in tropical rainforests   d. only in scientific experiments
25. One-hundredth of a meter is written as a ___ .
    a. decimeter   b. millimeter   (c.) centimeter   d. kilometer
26. How many millimeters make a centimeter?
    a. 100   (b.) 10   c. 1000   d. 0.10
27. A prefix meaning one thousand standard units is ___ .
    a. milli-   b. centi-   (c.) kilo-   d. deci-
28. On the Celsius scale, water boils at what temperature?
    a. 32 degrees   b. 212 degrees   c. 0 degrees   (d.) 100 degrees
29. 50 cc of water would equal which quantity?
    a. 5000 mL   b. 500 mL   (c.) 50 mL   d. 0.5 L
30. Which of the following units would we use to measure the distance to Australia?
    a. millimeters   b. centimeters   (c.) kilometers   d. kilograms

Page 5

THE COMPOUND MICROSCOPE   Name _____

Label each of the following parts on the diagram of a compound microscope. Describe the purpose/use of each part.

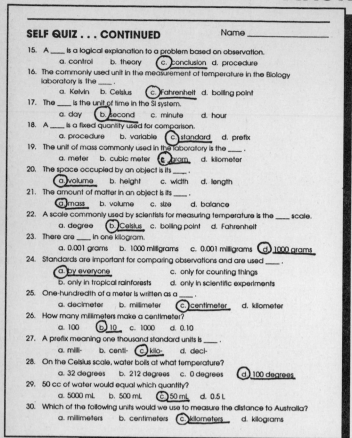

coarse adjustment
fine adjustment
arm
clip
diaphragm
base

eyepiece
body tube
nosepiece
high power obj.
low power obj.
stage
mirror

1. base—part on which the microscope rests
2. mirror—reflects light through objective lens into barrel of microscope
3. stage—surface on which slide is placed
4. arm—part by which microscope is carried
5. fine adjustment—used for fine, detailed focusing of microscope
6. coarse adjustment—used for focusing microscope
7. eyepiece—tube containing lens through which you look into microscope
8. body tube—tube extending from eyepiece to objectives
9. nosepiece—revolving circular structure containing objectives
10. high power objective—objective used for focusing minute details on microscope slide
11. low power objective—first objective used for focusing microscope slide
12. clip—used to hold slide on stage
13. diaphragm—controls amount of light that goes through stage into objective lens

Page 6

MICROSCOPE CROSSWORD   Name _____

```
    C
    L       L
H I G H P O W E R O B J E C T I V E
    P       O
    D I A P H R A G M   B A S E   N
        M   W       R       S   O
    F I N E A D J U S T M E N T   S
      R R   R       A       A   E
      R   O C U L A R       D   P
      O   B           J     U   I
      R   J           U     S   E
          E           S   T A G E
          C           T
  B O D Y T U B E     A R M
          I               E
          V               N
          E               T
```

Across
3. Lens that allows greater magnification
5. Regulates the amount of light
6. The microscope rests on this.
10. Used for final focusing
11. Eyepiece
12. Platform upon which to mount the slide
13. Holds eyepiece lens at top and objective lens at bottom
14. Holds the tube and stage and attaches them to the base

Down
1. Holds the slide in place
2. Lens used to locate the specimen
4. Used for first focusing
7. Rotating piece that holds objective lens
8. Reflects light to the specimen
9. Chemical sometimes used to make the specimen visible

Page 7

STATES OF MATTER   Name _____

Complete the following table by placing a check mark in each of the first three columns as it applies. Then, identify its state as solid, liquid or gas in the last column.

Example	Definite Shape	Definite Volume	Takes Shape of Container	State of Matter
1. water at 25°C		X	X	liquid
2. ice at -4°C	X	X		Solid
3. steam at 105°C			X	gas
4. iron	X	X		Solid
5. air			X	gas
6. carbon dioxide at 20°C			X	gas
7. juice		X	X	liquid
8. wood	X	X		Solid
9. oil		X	X	liquid
10. nitrogen at room temperature			X	gas
11. milk		X	X	liquid
12. ozone			X	gas
13. glass	X	X		Solid
14. coffee		X	X	liquid
15. chalk	X	X		solid

Page 8

CHEMICAL vs. PHYSICAL CHANGE   Name _____

In a physical change, the original substance still exists, it has only changed in form. Energy changes usually do not accompany physical changes, except in phase changes and when substances dissolve.

In a chemical change, a new substance is produced. Energy changes always accompany chemical changes. Physical changes usually accompany chemical changes.

Classify the following as being either a chemical or a physical change.

1. Sodium chloride dissolves in water. **physical**
2. Hydrochloric acid reacts with sodium hydroxide to produce a salt, water and heat. **chemical**
3. A pellet of sodium is sliced in half. **physical**
4. Water is heated and changed to steam. **physical**
5. Food is digested. **chemical**
6. Starch molecules are formed from smaller glucose molecules. **chemical**
7. Ice melts. **physical**
8. Plant leaves lose water through evaporation. **physical**
9. A red blood cell placed in distilled water will swell and burst. **physical**
10. The energy in food molecules is transferred into molecules of ATP. **chemical**
11. The roots of a plant absorb water. **physical**
12. Iron rusts. **chemical**
13. Oxygen is incorporated into hemoglobin to bring it to the cells. **chemical**
14. A person gets cooler by perspiring. **physical**
15. Proteins are made form amino acids. **chemical**
16. A match burns. **chemical**
17. A toothpick is broken in half. **physical**

ELEMENTS, COMPOUNDS AND MIXTURES   Name _____

An element consists of only one kind of atom. A compound consists of two or more different elements chemically combined in a fixed ratio. The components of a mixture can be in any proportion and are not chemically bound.

Classify each of the following as an element, compound or mixture by writing E, C or M in the space provided.

1. sodium **E**
2. water **C**
3. soil **M**
4. coffee **M**
5. oxygen **E**
6. alcohol **C**
7. carbon dioxide **C**
8. cake batter **M**
9. air **M**
10. soap **M**
11. iron **E**
12. salt water **M**
13. ice cream **M**
14. nitrogen **E**
15. eggs **M**
16. blood **M**
17. table salt **C**
18. nail polish **M**
19. milk **M**
20. cola **M**

21. orange juice **M**

22. helium **E**

23. methane **C**

ELEMENT SYMBOLS   Name _____

Write the symbol for the following elements which are common in living things.

1. oxygen **O**
2. hydrogen **H**
3. chlorine **Cl**
4. potassium **K**
5. fluorine **F**
6. manganese **Mn**
7. carbon **C**
8. zinc **Zn**
9. sodium **Na**
10. sulfur **S**
11. phosphorus **P**
12. iodine **I**
13. magnesium **Mg**
14. nitrogen **N**
15. copper **Cu**
16. iron **Fe**
17. calcium **Ca**
18. cobalt **Co**

Write the name of the element indicated by each of the following symbols.

19. As **arsenic**
20. Pb **lead**
21. Kr **krypton**
22. Ba **barium**
23. He **helium**
24. Ne **neon**
25. Si **silicon**
26. U **uranium**
27. Sn **tin**
28. Pt **plantinum**
29. Rn **radon**
30. Al **aluminum**
31. Cu **copper**
32. Ag **silver**
33. Pu **plutonium**
34. Sr **strontium**
35. Am **americium**
36. Au **gold**
37. Ra **radium**
38. Ge **germanium**
39. Br **bromine**
40. Hg **mercury**

PARTS OF THE ATOM   Name _____

Using the Periodic Table of the Elements, determine the number of protons, neutrons and electrons in each of the following atoms. Draw a model of the atom showing the electrons in the proper energy levels.

1. $_1^1H$ ___ protons **1** / ___ neutrons **0** / ___ electrons **1**

2. $_6^{12}C$ ___ protons **6** / ___ neutrons **6** / ___ electrons **6**

3. $_{11}^{23}Na$ ___ protons **11** / ___ neutrons **12** / ___ electrons **11**

4. $_{15}^{31}P$ ___ protons **15** / ___ neutrons **16** / ___ electrons **15**

5. $_8^{16}O$ ___ protons **8** / ___ neutrons **8** / ___ electrons **8**

IONIC vs. COVALENT BONDS

Name _____

When nonmetals chemically bond they do so by sharing electrons. The bond is called a covalent bond. When an active metal and a nonmetal bond, the active metal transfers one or more electrons to the nonmetal. This bond is called an ionic bond. Ionic compounds (except for bases) are also called salts.

Classify the following compounds as ionic or covalent.

1. $CaCl_2$ — ionic
2. CO_2 — covalent
3. H_2O — covalent
4. $BaCl_2$ — ionic
5. O_2 — covalent
6. NaF — ionic
7. NaS — ionic
8. S_8 — covalent
9. SO_3 — covalent
10. $LiBr$ — ionic
11. MgO — ionic
12. C_2H_5OH — covalent
13. HCl — covalent

14. N_2 — covalent
15. NaI — ionic
16. NO_2 — covalent
17. Al_2O_3 — ionic
18. $FeCl_3$ — ionic
19. P_2O_5 — covalent
20. N_2O_3 — covalent
21. H_2 — covalent
22. K_2O — ionic
23. KI — ionic
24. P_4 — covalent
25. CH_4 — covalent
26. $NaCl$ — ionic

Draw an electron shell diagram of the ionic compound calcium oxide, CaO.

Draw an electron shell diagram of the covalent compound methane, CH_4.

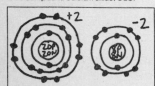

Page 13

BALANCING EQUATIONS

Name _____

Balance the following chemical equations.

1. $2 Na + I_2 \rightarrow 2 NaI$
2. $2 N_2 + O_2 \rightarrow 2 N_2O$
3. $N_2 + 3 H_2 \rightarrow 2 NH_3$
4. $CH_4 + 2 O_2 \rightarrow CO_2 + 2 H_2O$
5. $2 KI + Cl_2 \rightarrow 2 KCl + I_2$
6. $2 S + 3 O_2 \rightarrow 2 SO_3$
7. $2 H_2O_2 \rightarrow 2 H_2O + O_2$
8. $2 Na + 2 H_2O \rightarrow 2 NaOH + H_2$
9. $2 H_2O \rightarrow 2 H_2 + O_2$
10. $2 KClO_3 \rightarrow 2 KCl + 3 O_2$
11. $K_3PO_4 + 3 HCl \rightarrow 3 KCl + H_3PO_4$
12. $CO_2 + H_2O \rightarrow H_2CO_3$
13. $K_2O + H_2O \rightarrow 2 KOH$
14. $Mg + 2 HCl \rightarrow MgCl_2 + H_2$
15. $2 KOH + H_2SO_4 \rightarrow K_2SO_4 + 2 H_2O$

Page 14

SELF QUIZ—ATOMIC STRUCTURE AND EQUATIONS

Name _____

Circle the letter of the correct answer.

1. A(n) ____ is a substance made up of one kind of atom.
   a. compound   **b. element**   c. mixture   d. enzyme
2. The smallest particle of a element having the properties of that element is a(n) ____.
   a. atom   b. compound   **c. molecule**   d. enzyme
3. A(n) ____ is matter made of substances that are not chemically bonded together.
   a. mixture   b. element   c. compound   d. molecule
4. The correctly written symbol for chlorine is ____.
   a. C   b. CL   c. Ch   **d. Cl**
5. How many atoms of hydrogen are in each molecule of table sugar, $C_{12}H_{22}O_{11}$?
   a. 11   b. 12   **c. 22**   d. 45
6. Which of the following is a compound?
   a. iron   b. blood   **c. carbon dioxide**   d. air
7. A(n) ____ contains two or more atoms bonded together.
   a. mixture   **b. molecule**   c. atom   d. element
8. A substance that contains two or more different kinds of atoms bonded together is ____.
   a. an element   b. oxygen   c. energy   **d. a compound**
9. How may atoms of oxygen are represented in the equation: $C + O_2 \rightarrow CO_2$?
   a. 1   **b. 2**   c. 3   d. 4
10. The smallest part of a compound that still has the properties of that compound is a(n) ____.
    a. atom   b. cell   **c. molecule**   d. element
11. An atom that contains 15 protons and 10 neutrons within its nucleus will have an atomic mass of ____ amu.
    a. 5   b. 10   c. 15   **d. 25**
12. An atom of atomic number 12 and mass number 22 contains how many protons?
    a. 10   **b. 12**   c. 22   d. 34
13. The atom described in Problem 12 will have how many electrons?
    a. 10   **b. 12**   c. 22   d. 34
14. The atom described in Problem 12 will have how many neutrons?
    a. 10   b. 12   c. 22   d. 34
15. Elements combine by losing, sharing or gaining ____.
    a. electrons   b. protons   c. neutrons   d. molecules

Page 15

ACID, BASE OR SALT?

Name _____

Classify each of the following as an acid, a base or a salt.

1. HNO_3 — acid
2. $NaOH$ — base
3. $NaNO_3$ — salt
4. HCl — acid
5. KCl — salt
6. $Ba(OH)_2$ — base
7. KOH — base
8. H_2S — acid
9. $Al(NO_2)_3$ — salt
10. H_2SO_4 — acid
11. $CaCl_2$ — salt
12. H_3PO_4 — acid
13. Na_2SO_4 — salt
14. $Mg(OH)_2$ — base
15. H_2CO_3 — acid
16. NH_4OH — base
17. NH_4Cl — salt
18. HBr — acid
19. $FeBr_3$ — salt
20. HF — acid
21. $NaCl$ — salt
22. $Ca(OH)_2$ — base
23. $HC_2H_3O_2$ — acid
24. $CuCl_2$ — salt
25. HNO_2 — acid

26. $NaHCO_3$ — salt

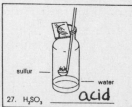

27. H_2SO_3 — acid

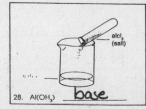

28. $Al(OH)_3$ — base

Page 16

ANSWER KEY

pH

Name _____

pH is as scale that measures the hydronium ion concentration of a solution. A pH of less than 7 indicates an acidic solution. A solution with a pH of 7 is neutral. A solution with a pH of 7 to 14 is basic and contains a higher concentration of hydroxide ions than hydronium ions.

Indicators are substances that change color in the presence of certain irons. Phenolphthalein is colorless in an acid and a neutral solution, pink in a base. Litmus is red in a acid, blue in a base.

For each of the following substances indicate the pH range expected: acid = pH < 7, neutral = pH = 7, or base = pH > 7 Indicate the color the indicator will appear, and state the solution's use.

Solution	pH Range	Phenol-phtalein	Blue Litmus	Red Litmus	Use
vinegar	< 7	colorless	red	red	pickling
soap	> 7	pink	blue	blue	cleaning
cola	< 7	colorless	red	red	drinking/digestion
ammonia	> 7	'pink	blue	blue	cleaning
rain	< 7	colorless	red	red	replenishing H_2O supply
Milk of Magnesia	> 7	pink	blue	blue	combat heartburn
milk	< 7	colorless	red	red	provides Ca
saliva	< 7	colorless	red	red	begins digestion of carbohydrates
coffee	< 7	colorless	red	red	drinking
gastric juices	< 7	colorless	red	red	break down food
human blood	> 7	pink	blue	blue	transport oxygen
orange juice	< 7	colorless	red	red	nutrition
Kool-Aid	= 7	colorless	blue	red	nutrition
drain cleaner	> 7	pink	blue	blue	dissolves oil, soap, etc.
bleach	< 7	colorless	red	red	killing bacteria, whitening
shampoo	> 7	pink	blue	blue	cleaning, dissolving oils

Page 17

INORGANIC vs. ORGANIC COMPOUNDS

Name _____

Matter is often classified as organic or inorganic. Indicate the class for each type of matter. Then, identify it major properties as that of a salt, acid, base, protein, lipid, nucleic acid or carbohydrate.

Matter	Class	Properties of
1. HCl	inorganic	acid
2. DNA	organic	nucleic acid
3. starch	organic	carbohydrate
4. KOH	inorganic	base
5. sodium chloride	inorganic	salt
6. skin	organic	protein
7. animal fat	organic	lipid
8. glucose	organic	carbohydrate
9. vegetable oil	organic	lipid
10. hair	organic	protein
11. RNA	organic	nucleic acid
12. sucrose	organic	carbohydrate
13. butter	organic	lipid
14. fingernails	organic	protein
15. H_2SO_4	inorganic	acid
16. HNO_3	inorganic	acid
17. gelatin	organic	protein
18. molasses	organic	carbohydrate
19. vinegar	organic	acid

Page 18

DEHYDRATION SYNTHESIS

Name _____

In the following two examples of dehydration synthesis, show how the removal of the water molecule(s) takes place by drawing a ring around the components of water. Then, draw the structural formula of each product.

Synthesis of a Fat

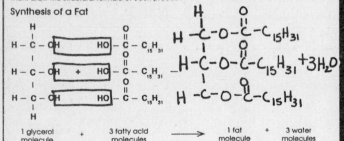

| 1 glycerol molecule | + | 3 fatty acid molecules | ⟶ | 1 fat molecule | + | 3 water molecules |

Formation of a Peptide Bond

amino acid   +   amino acid   ⟶

dipeptide   +   water

Page 19

HYDROLYSIS

Name _____

Hydrolysis is the opposite of a dehydration synthesis. A large molecule is broken down into two or more smaller molecules by the addition of water.

Draw the structural formulas of the expected products in the two following hydrolysis reactions.

Breakdown of a Disaccharide to Monosaccharides

Disaccharide   + H_2O maltase ⟶

2 Monosaccharides

Breakdown of a Lipid

lipid   +   3 water molecules   lipase ⟶   glycerol   3 fatty acids

Page 20

ANSWER KEY

DIFFUSIONS AND OSMOSIS

Name _____

The diagrams below show what each solution would look like after a period of time has passed. Label each as osmosis or diffusion.

diffusion

semipermeable membrane

osmosis

semipermeable membrane

osmosis

Key
○ = salt molecule
● = water molecule

Page 21

LIFE ACTIVITIES AND BODY SYSTEMS

Name _____

Match the life activity in Column I with its example in Column II.

Column I

1. nutrition — **c**
2. circulation — **e**
3. respiration — **b**
4. excretion — **f**
5. synthesis — **d**
6. regulation — **h**
7. growth — **k**
8. reproduction — **a**
9. metabolism — **j**
10. homeostasis — **g**
11. digestion — **i**

Column II

a. a cat has a litter of six kittens
b. the cells utilize glucose to produce energy
c. a plant absorbs minerals form the soil
d. a plant forms large starch molecules form smaller sugar molecules
e. the bloodstream brings oxygen and food to the cells
f. waste products are eliminated during perspiration
g. a person sweats to keep body temperature at a safe level
h. the brain coordinates the various systems of the body
i. process by which food is changed into form the body can use
j. the human body produces hormones, vitamins, proteins, enzymes, etc. to keep it functioning
k. a 7-pound baby becomes a 180-pound man

Fill in the blanks with the correct body systems.

The lungs are the main organ of the **respiratory** system, but they are also an organ in the **excretory** system. The lymph and the lymphatics are part of the **circulatory** system. Although food does not pass through the liver and gall bladder, they are part of the **digestive** system. As a duct gland, the pancreas is part of the **digestive** system. As a ductless gland, the pancreas is part of the **endocrine** system. The hypothalamus, through its neurosecretory cells, coordinate the activities of the **endocrine** and **nervous** systems.

Page 22

LIFE ACTIVITIES CROSSWORD

Name _____

Across

1. process of producing more organisms in order to continue the species
5. information acquired by chemical stimuli or response to the environment that is directed to the brain
6. a chemical messenger that is produced in one part of an organism and triggers a reaction in another part of the organism
7. Response of the body to invasion of foreign substances
11. The result of sensory, neural, and hormonal factors in response to changes in external or internal conditions
14. The ingestion of food for energy and to provide vitamins and minerals the body cannot make for itself
15. The breakdown of foods into molecules the body can use
16. Distribution of materials within an organism

Down

1. The utilization of oxygen and release of carbon dioxide
2. System that relays commands to skeletal muscles and stimulates glands and other muscle so the organism may continue to live and respond to stimuli
3. Ability to independently move about form place to place
4. Series of changes, beginning with conception, an organism undergoes until the adult stage is reached
8. The sum of all chemical processes within a living cell or organism
9. The state required by all organisms in order to maintain the proper salt balance
10. The transport of material form one place to another within an organism through the use of internal fluid
12. An organism's increase in size or number of cells, with no developmental changes
13. Control and coordination of all the activities of an organism

Crossword solution:
REPRODUCTION
SENSORY HORMONE
IMMUNITY
BEHAVIOR
REGULATION NUTRITION
DIGESTION
TRANSPORT
(with down entries: RESPIRATION, METABOLISM, LOCOMOTION, DEVELOPMENT, WATER, CIRCULATION, GROWTH, HOMEOSTASIS)

Page 23

AUTOTROPHS VS. HETEROTROPHS

Name _____

An autotroph is an organism that is capable of forming organic compounds form inorganic compounds in it environment. In other words, an autotroph can make its own food. Heterotrophs must get their food from other organisms.

Classify the following organisms as an autotroph (a) or a heterotroph (h).

1. maple tree — **a**
2. human — **h**
3. wheat — **a**
4. fungi — **h**
5. ameba — **h**
6. green algae — **a**
7. housefly — **h**
8. fern — **a**
9. dandelion — **a**
10. goldfish — **h**

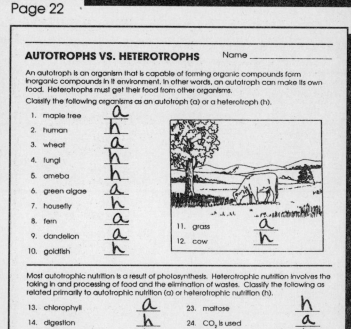

11. grass — **a**
12. cow — **h**

Most autotrophic nutrition is a result of photosynthesis. Heterotrophic nutrition involves the taking in and processing of food and the elimination of wastes. Classify the following as related primarily to autotrophic nutrition (a) or heterotrophic nutrition (h).

13. chlorophyll — **a**
14. digestion — **h**
15. phagocytosis — **h**
16. photolysis — **a**
17. rhizoids — **h**
18. lipase — **h**
19. carbon fixation — **a**
20. pseudopods — **h**
21. PGAL — **a**
22. light reaction — **a**

23. maltose — **h**
24. CO_2 is used — **a**
25. ingestion — **h**
26. chloroplasts — **a**
27. dark reaction — **a**
28. grana — **a**
29. proteose — **h**
30. glucose production — **a**
31. stroma — **a**
32. bile — **h**

Page 24

ANSWER KEY

ANIMAL CELLS

Name _____

Label the organelles in the diagram below of a typical animal cell. Describe the function/purpose of each organelle in the cell.

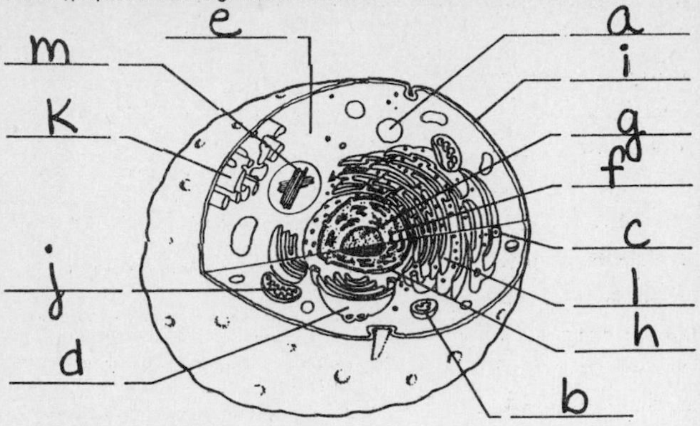

a. vacuole—bubblelike storage structure
b. lysosome—digests large particles
c. ribosomes—structures in which proteins are manufactured
d. Golgi complex—area that stores and packages chemicals
e. cytoplasm—materials between nucleus and cell membrane
f. nucleus—control center containing genetic information
g. nucleolus—spherical body in the nucleus
h. nuclear membrane—membrane surrounding nucleus
i. cell (plasma) membrane—membrane around outside of cell
j. mitochondria—release energy from nutrients
k. smooth endoplasmic reticulum—cell's internal transport system
l. rough endoplasmic reticulum—endoplasmic reticulum with ribosomes attached
m. centriole—small, dark body outside nucleus used during cell division

PLANT CELLS

Name _____

Label the organelles in the diagram below of a typical plant cell. Describe the function/purpose of each organelle in the cell.

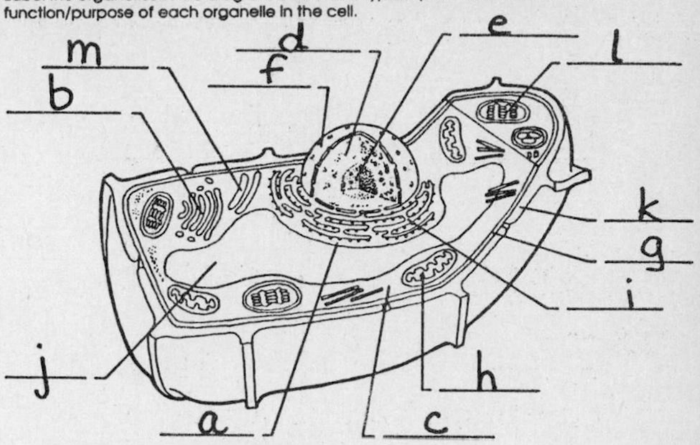

a. ribosomes—structures in which proteins are manufactured
b. Golgi complex—area that stores and packages chemicals
c. cytoplasm—materials between nucleus and cell membrane
d. nucleus—control center containing genetic information
e. nucleolus—spherical body in the nucleus
f. nuclear membrane—membrane surrounding nucleus
g. cell (plasma) membrane—membrane surrounding cytoplasm and organelles
h. mitochondria—releases energy from nutrients
i. rough endoplasmic reticulum—endoplasmic reticulum with ribosomes attached
j. vacuole—bubblelike storage structure
k. cell wall—stiff outer covering of plant cell
l. chloroplast—plastid that stores chlorophyll used in photosynthesis
m. smooth endoplasmic reticulum—cell's internal transport system

FUNCTION OF THE ORGANELLES

Name _____

Which organelle performs each of the following functions within the cell?

Function	Organelle
1. Controls the movement into and out of the cell	1. cell (plasma) membrane
2. Watery material which contains many of the materials involved in cell metabolism	2. cytoplasm
3. Serves as a pathway for the transport of materials throughout the cell; also associate with synthesis and storage	3. endoplasmic reticulum
4. Serves as the control center for cell metabolism and reproduction	4. nucleus
5. Sites of protein synthesis	5. ribosomes
6. Involved in the digestion of food within the cell	6. lysosomes
7. The "powerhouse" of the cell	7. mitochondria
8. Packages and secretes the products of the cell	8. Golgi bodies
9. Involved in cell division in animal cells	9. centrioles
10. Fluid filled organelles enclosed by a membrane, contains stored food or wastes	10. vacuoles
11. Site of the production of ribosomes	11. nucleolus
12. Controls movement into and out of the nucleus	12. nuclear membrane
13. Gives the cell its shape and provides protection; not found in animal cells	13. cell wall
14. Hairlike structures with the capacity for movement	14. cilia
15. A long, hairlike structure used for movement	15. flagellum
16. Site of photosynthesis	16. chloroplast
17. During cytokinesis, the new cell wall that begins to form in the middle, dividing the two sides	17. cell plate
18. rod-shaped bodies that carry genetic information	18. chromosomes

PARTS OF THE CELL—MATCHING

Name _____

Match the descriptions in Column I with the name in Column II.

Column I	Column II
g 1. holds nucleus together	a. Golgi bodies
f 2. surface for chemical activity	b. nucleus
p 3. units of heredity	c. chromosomes
o 4. digestion center	d. vacuole
e 5. where proteins are made	e. ribosomes
h 6. structures involved in mitosis in animal cells only	f. endoplasmic reticulum
t 7. microscopic cylinders that support and give the cell shape	g. nuclear membrane
m 8. shapes and supports a plant cell	h. centrioles
a 9. stores and releases chemicals	i. cytoplasm
k 10. food for plant cells is made here	j. chlorophyll
r 11. spherical body within nucleus	k. chloroplasts
l 12. controls entry into and out of cell	l. cell (plasma) membrane
j 13. traps light and is used to produce food for plants	m. cell wall
b 14. chromosomes are found here	n. mitochondria
i 15. jellylike substance within cell	o. lysosome
c 16. contains code which guides all cell activities	p. genes
q 17. minute hole in nuclear membrane	q. nuclear pore
n 18. "powerhouse" of cell	r. nucleolus
d 19. contains water and dissolved minerals	s. plastid
s 20. stores food or contains pigment	t. microtubule

ANSWER KEY

STAGES OF MITOSIS
Name _____

Number the following six diagrams of the stages of mitosis in animal cells in the proper order. Label each stage with the proper name.

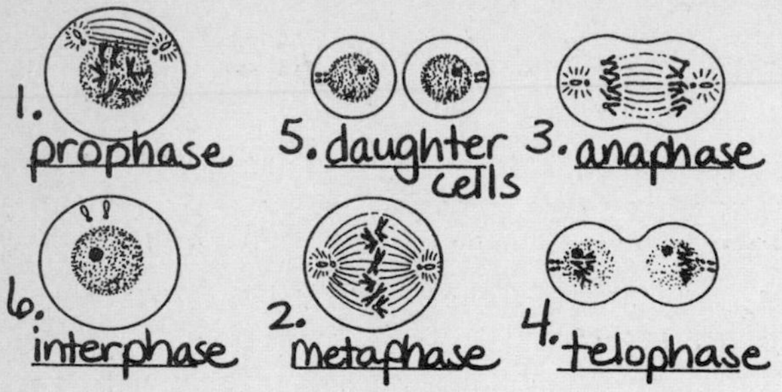

1. prophase
5. daughter cells
3. anaphase
6. interphase
2. metaphase
4. telophase

Do the same for the following diagrams of mitosis in plant cells.

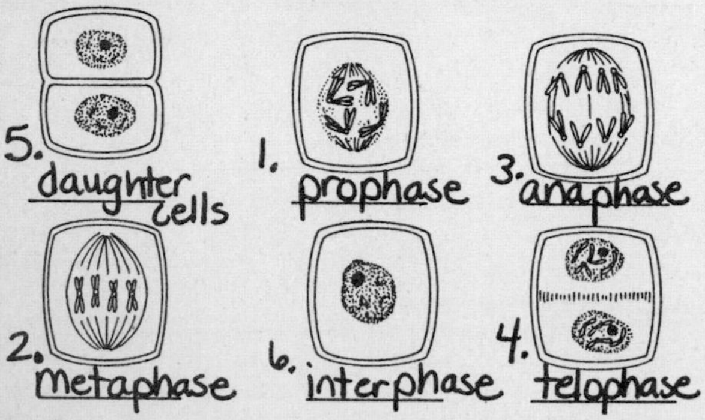

5. daughter cells
1. prophase
3. anaphase
2. metaphase
6. interphase
4. telophase

STAGES OF MEIOSIS
Name _____

Number the following diagram of a first meiotic division in the proper order. Label each phase correctly as prophase I, metaphase I, anaphase I or telophase I.

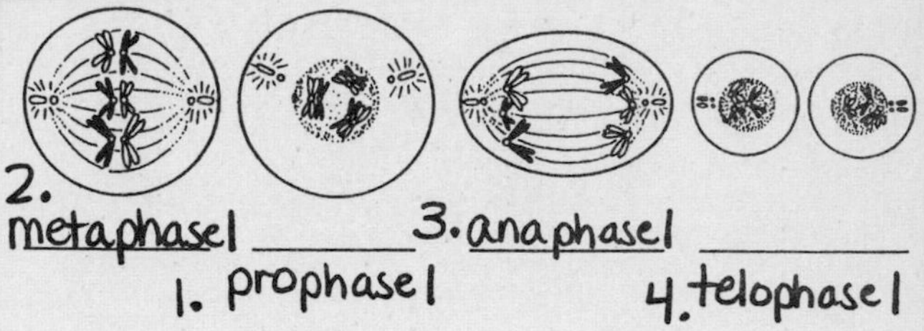

2. metaphase I
3. anaphase I
1. prophase I
4. telophase I

So the same for the diagram of the second meiotic division. Label each phase correctly as prophase II, metaphase II, anaphase II, telophase II

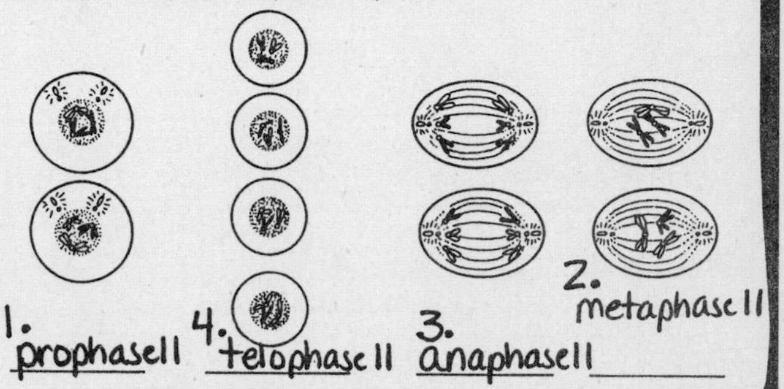

1. prophase II
4. telophase II
3. anaphase II
2. metaphase II

COMPARING MITOSIS AND MEIOSIS
Name _____

Determine whether the following characteristics apply to mitosis, meiosis or both by putting a check in the appropriate column(s).

	Mitosis	Meiosis
1. no pairing of homologs occurs	X	
2. two divisions		X
3. four daughter cells produced		X
4. associated with growth and asexual reproduction	X	
5. associated with sexual reproduction		X
6. one division	X	
7. two daughter cells produced	X	
8. involves duplication of chromosomes	X	X
9. chromosome number is maintained	X	
10. chromosome number is halved		X
11. crossing over between homologous chromosomes may occur		X
12. daughter cells are identical to parent cell	X	
13. daughter cells are not identical to parent cell		X
14. produces gametes		X
15. synapsis occurs in prophase		X

TYPES OF ASEXUAL REPRODUCTION
Name _____

Label the following diagrams of types of asexual reproduction as binary fission, budding, sporulation, regeneration, parthenogenesis or vegetative propagation. Give two examples of organisms that use each method of reproduction.

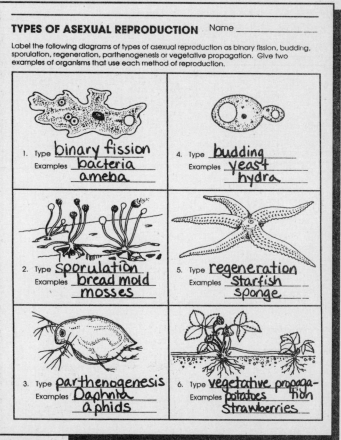
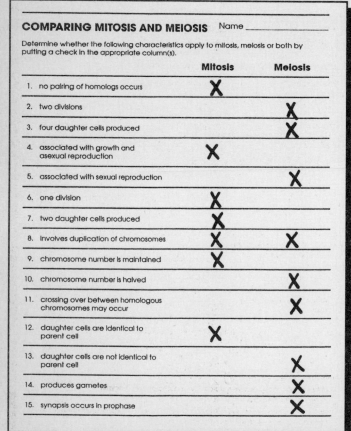

1. Type binary fission
   Examples bacteria
   ameba

4. Type budding
   Examples yeast
   hydra

2. Type sporulation
   Examples bread mold
   mosses

5. Type regeneration
   Examples starfish
   sponge

3. Type parthenogenesis
   Examples Daphnia
   aphids

6. Type vegetative propagation
   Examples potatoes
   strawberries

CELLULAR RESPIRATION

Name _____

Fill in the blanks in the following sequences:

Glycolysis Respiration

glucose + **2** ATP $\xrightarrow{\text{enzymes}}$ 2 **pyruvic acid** + **4** ATP

Anaerobic Respiration

2 pyruvic acid $\longrightarrow$ 2 **lactic acid**

or

2 pyruvic acid $\longrightarrow$ 2 **alcohol** + 2 **carbon dioxide**

Aerobic Respiration

2 pyruvic acid + oxygen $\xrightarrow{\text{enzymes}}$ **carbon dioxide** **water** + **34** ATP

Fill in the blanks with the correct term in the questions below.

1. Glycolysis produces a net gain of **2** ATP molecules per molecule of glucose by an anaerobic reaction.

2. Aerobic respiration produces a net gain of **34** ATP molecules per molecule of glucose.

3. **Aerobic** respiration is a more efficient producer of energy than an aerobic respiration.

4. The energy contained in a molecule of glucose is changed to a more usable form by combining a **phosphorus** atom with **ADP** to form ATP.

5. When ATP is broken down to **ADP** and **phosphorus**, energy is **released**.

6. During glycolysis, glucose is first split into two molecules of **PGAL**. This requires the energy released from two molecules of ATP being converted to two molecules of **ADP**.

7. The **PGAL** is then converted to **pyruvic acid**, producing four **ADP** molecules and two **NADH** molecules, which are part of the electron transport chain.

8. The **electron** transport chain, which supplies the energy needed for the formation of ATP, requires the formation of **NADH** from NAD$^+$, and **FADH$_2$** from FAD.

9. The hydrogen necessary in this chain comes from the breaking apart of **water** molecules.

10. The oxygen released is used to form **CO$_2$**.

CLASSIFICATION

Name _____

Number the seven major classification groups in order from the one containing the largest number of organisms to that containing the least.

4 order   **2** phylum

5 family   **7** species

1 kingdom   **3** class

6 genus

On the chart below, classify the five kingdoms according to the characteristic in the left-hand column.

Characteristic	Monera	Protista	Fungi	Plantae	Animalia
cell type (prokaryotic/ eukaryotic)	prokaryotic	eukaryotic	eukaryotic	eukaryotic	eukaryotic
number of cells (unicellular/ multicellular)	unicellular	unicellular	most multicellular	multicellular	multicellular
cell nucleus (present/ absent)	absent	present	present	present	present
cell wall (present/ absent)	present	present in some	present	present	absent
cell wall composition	polysaccharides and amino acids	varies	chitin	cellulose	—
nutrition (autotrophic/ heterotrophic)	autotrophic/ heterotrophic	autotrophic/ heterotrophic	heterotrophic	autotrophic	heterotrophic
locomotion (present/ absent)	present in some	present in some	absent	absent	present

CLASSIFYING ORGANISMS

Name _____

The drawings below show 15 different organisms. Give the name of each organism. Then, indicate the phylum to which it belongs.

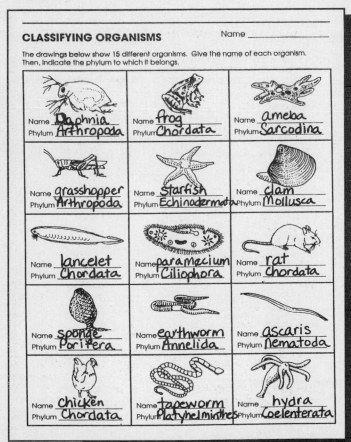

Name **Daphnia** Phylum **Arthropoda**

Name **frog** Phylum **Chordata**

Name **ameba** Phylum **Sarcodina**

Name **grasshopper** Phylum **Arthropoda**

Name **starfish** Phylum **Echinodermata**

Name **clam** Phylum **Mollusca**

Name **lancelet** Phylum **Chordata**

Name **paramecium** Phylum **Ciliophora**

Name **rat** Phylum **Chordata**

Name **sponge** Phylum **Porifera**

Name **earthworm** Phylum **Annelida**

Name **ascaris** Phylum **Nematoda**

Name **chicken** Phylum **Chordata**

Name **tapeworm** Phylum **Platyhelminthes**

Name **hydra** Phylum **Coelenterata**

NUTRITION IN PROTOZOANS

Name _____

Label the following parts on the diagrams below of an ameba. State the function/purpose of each part.

a. food vacuole—used for digestion and temporary storage

b. pseudopods—temporary footlike projection used in locomotion

c. nucleus—control center of the cell

d. contractile vacuole—gets rid of excess water and wastes

e. cell membrane—outside boundary of the cell

f. ectoplasm—thin layer of cytoplasm under cell membrane

g. endoplasm—thick cytoplasm that fills the cell

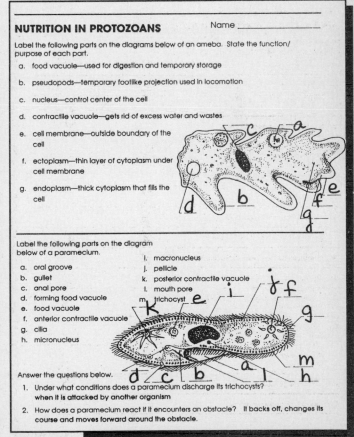

Label the following parts on the diagram below of a paramecium.

a. oral groove
b. gullet
c. anal pore
d. forming food vacuole
e. food vacuole
f. anterior contractile vacuole
g. cilia
h. micronucleus

i. macronucleus
j. pellicle
k. posterior contractile vacuole
l. mouth pore
m. trichocyst

Answer the questions below.

1. Under what conditions does a paramecium discharge its trichocysts? **when it is attacked by another organism**

2. How does a paramecium react if it encounters an obstacle? **It backs off, changes its course and moves forward around the obstacle.**

ANSWER KEY

NUTRITION IN HYDRA

Name _____

Label the following parts of the hydra on the diagram below. State the function/purpose of each part.

a. mouth—only opening of gastrovascular cavity

b. tentacle—armlike structures around the mouth, armed with nematocysts

c. gastrovascular cavity—interior of hollow body

d. nematocysts—stinging structures used to capture small animals

e. basal disk—used to attach hydra to rock or water plant

f. egg—female reproductive cell

g. ovary—female reproductive organ that produces eggs

h. sperm—male reproductive cell

i. testis—male reproductive organ that produces sperm

j. bud—projection used for asexual reproduction

k. mesoglea—jellylike layer between the inner and outer layers of the body

Fill in the blanks with the correct answers.

The **tentacles** move food through the **mouth** into the gastrovascular, or digestive, cavity. When the lining of the digestive cavity secretes **enzymes** the food is broken up into tiny pieces. The partly digested food is then engulfed by special cells in the lining that **digest** them further. Any undigested or indigestible material is egested through the **mouth**.

MATCHING—CLASSIFICATION AND PROTISTS

Name _____

Match the definition in Column I with the correct word in Column II (not all words will be used).

Column I

c 1. method of sexual reproduction in paramecia

e 2. protozoan with short, hairlike structures used for movement

a 3. fingerlike projections of cytoplasm

d 4. protozoan that has a 3-stage life cycle

k 5. largest category in a kingdom

b 6. first word in a scientific name

j 7. science of classifying living things

i 8. smallest category in a kingdom

f 9. division of a class

h 10. method of reproduction in an ameba

Column II

a. pseudopod
b. genus
c. conjugation
d. slime mold
e. paramecium
f. order
g. class
h. fission
i. species
j. taxonomy
k. phylum

Match the following functions to the correct organelle.

f 1. gives shape to the paramecium and euglena

c 2. controls sexual reproduction in the paramecium

e 3. used for excretion of waste products

b 4. contains chlorophyll

i 5. reacts to light

g 6. used for movement by the euglena

k 7. controls metabolism of a paramecium

a 8. used for movement by a paramecium

d 9. The paramecium ingests its food through this opening.

a. cilia
b. chloroplast
c. micronucleus
d. oral groove
e. contractile vacuole
f. pellicle
g. flagellum
h. cytostome
i. eyespot
j. pseudopod
k. macronucleus

SELF QUIZ—CLASSIFICATION AND PROTISTS

Name _____

Circle the letter of the correct answer.

1. Of the following groups, a ____ contains animals that are least alike.
   a. family b. phylum c. division d. class
2. Which of the following groupings contain the most closely related organisms?
   a. family b. phylum c. genus d. kingdom
3. Which of the following is a correctly written scientific name?
   a. Panthera Leo b. panthera leo c. PANTHERA LEO d. Panthera leo
4. The smallest category of a kingdom is a(n) ____.
   a. division b. species c. phylum d. genus
5. ____ is the science of classifying living things.
   a. Astronomy b. Biology c. Taxonomy d. Zoology
6. The cat and dog belong to the same order but different:
   a. kingdoms b. classes c. families d. divisions
7. Living things are usually classified into five:
   a. phyla b. kingdoms c. classes d. divisions
8. Which of the following is a Felis domesticus?
   a. horse b. house cat c. house finch d. lion
9. What language is used for scientific names?
   a. English b. Swedish c. German d. Latin
10. Organisms are classified into the group with which they share the most ____.
    a. food b. territory c. characteristics d. time
11. Why does each organism have a specific scientific name?
    a. for ease of study and communication c. name contains important information
    b. classification is less involved d. easier to alphabetize all organisms
12. Protozoans and slime molds belong to a group of organisms known as ____.
    a. protists b. fungi c. lichens d. parasites
13. The fingerlike projections of cytoplasm used by some protozoans for movement and obtaining food are:
    a. hyphae b. sporangia c. pseudopods d. oral grooves
14. A protist that has chlorophyll and produces its own food is a(n) ____ protist.
    a. plantlike b. sporozoan c. animallike d. saprophyte
15. A protist covered with many, short hairlike structures used for movement is a ____.
    a. parasite b. ciliate c. flagellate d. lichen
16. Which of the following protists have shells made of silica?
    a. diatoms b. ciliates c. ameba d. paramecia
17. The kingdom with one-celled organisms that are plantlike, animallike and funguslike is:
    a. ameba b. protozoa c. protista d. fungi
18. The long, hairlike structures protists use for locomotion are ____.
    a. ciliates b. flagellates c. amebas d. slime molds
19. One stage of a slime mold is:
    a. stage with a hard outer shell of chitin c. slimy mass stag like an ameba
    b. free swimming ciliate stage d. chloroplast stage
20. Euglena may obtain food by making it, but Ameba obtains food ____.
    a. by fermentation b. by surrounding it c. along an oral groove d. from a host

SELF QUIZ—VIRUSES

Name _____

Fill in the blanks from the word list below.

AIDS	antibodies	cells	interferon
measles	mumps	protein	reproduction
vaccines	weakened		

1. Viruses consist of nucleic acids covered by a coat of **protein**.
2. Viruses, unlike bacteria, are not composed of **cells**.
3. The only life function viruses can perform is **reproduction**.
4. Protection against some viral diseases can be produced by **vaccines**.
5. Name three viral diseases: **AIDS** **mumps** and **measles**.
6. A vaccine is made from a **weakened** form of the virus.
7. Two natural defenses the body has against viruses are **interferon** and **antibodies**.

Below are diagrams of three different types of viruses. Label the nucleic acid and protein coat in the polyhedral and rod-shaped viruses. Label the capsid, collar, tail sheath, tail fiber and base plate in the bacteriophage.

protein coat

nucleic acid
polyhedral virus

capsid
collar
tail
sheath
tail fiber
base plate
bacteriophage

protein coat

nucleic acid
rod-shaped virus

ANSWER KEY

BACTERIA—TYPICAL MONERANS

Name _____

Structure of Bacteria

Label the parts of a moneran on the diagram below. State the function/purpose of each.

a. flagella—long, whiplike structures used for movement _____

b. ribosomes—tiny organelles in which proteins are manufactured _____

c. nucleoid—region of cell in which DNA is concentrated

d. cell wall—tough outer layer that gives shape to the bacteria

e. cell (plasma) membrane—thin layer just inside the cell wall

f. capsule—layer of slime surrounding the cell wall

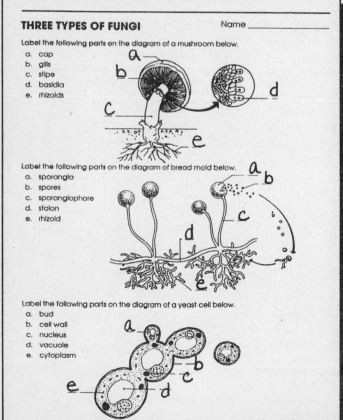

Conjugation in Bacteria

The diagrams below shows conjugation, a means of genetic transfer but not reproduction in bacteria. During conjugation, a plasmid is transferred from a donor to a recipient bacterium. Label the donor bacterium, the recipient bacterium, the plasmid and the cytoplasmic bridge on the diagrams.

donor bacterium   recipient bacterium
plasmid
cytoplasmic bridge

Answer the questions below.

1. By what process do bacteria reproduce?
   binary fission

2. What structures do some bacteria form under unfavorable conditions?
   spores

3. What do the monerans lack in their cell structure that is present in most other organisms? **nucleus**

4. Are the monerans prokaryotic or eukaryotic?
   prokaryotic

Page 41

SELF QUIZ—MONERANS

Name _____

Put the correct answer to the questions in the blanks using the words from the list below.

1. Monerans have no definite **nucleus**, but can still carry on reproduction.
2. Monerans have no **mitochondria** but can still carry on cellular respiration.
3. Cyanobacteria may also be called **blue-green algae**
4. When cyanobacteria multiply rapidly in a pond, they use up all the **oxygen**
5. Bacteria come in what three shapes? **round**, **rodlike**, **spiral**
6. Some bacteria have a whiplike tail called a **flagellum**
7. Bacteria that do not need oxygen to live are called **anaerobes**
8. Bacteria reproduce by what process? **binary fission**
9. Bacteria that live on dead organic matter are called **saprophytes**
10. Relationship between two organisms that do not harm either one **mutualism**
11. Two conditions bacteria need to live: **proper temperature, moisture**
12. Four ways we have of controlling bacterial growth. **refrigeration, freezing, canning, radiation**
13. **Bacteria** are the oldest known and simplest organism.
14. **Nitrogen fixing** bacteria live in nodules on the roots of plants, fixing atmospheric nitrogen, thus making it available for their own metabolic activities.
15. **Mutation** is the most important source of variability in bacteria.
16. Many scientists have suggested that **archaebacteria** should be considered a separate kingdom because they are remarkable different from all the bacteria.
17. **Actinomycetes** are the source of a majority, over 2000 kinds, of antibiotics.
18. **Spirochetes** are the causative agents of syphilis and Lyme disease.
19. **Chemosynthetic** bacteria depend on chemical sources—ammonia, methane and hydrogen sulfide—for energy for their metabolism.
20. **Cyanobacteria** were probably responsible for the accumulation of limestone deposits known as stromatolites.

actinomycetes	anaerobes	archaebacteria	binary fission	bacteria
blue-green algae	canning	chemosynthetic	cyanobactyeria	flagellum
freezing	mitochondria	moisture	mutation	mutualism
nitrogen fixing	nucleus	oxygen	proper temperature	radiation
refrigeration	round	rodlike	saprophytes	spiral	spirochetes

Page 42

THREE TYPES OF FUNGI

Name _____

Label the following parts on the diagram of a mushroom below.

a. cap
b. gills
c. stipe
d. basidia
e. rhizoids

Label the following parts on the diagram of bread mold below.

a. sporangia
b. spores
c. sporangiophore
d. stolon
e. rhizoid

Label the following parts on the diagram of a yeast cell below.

a. bud
b. cell wall
c. nucleus
d. vacuole
e. cytoplasm

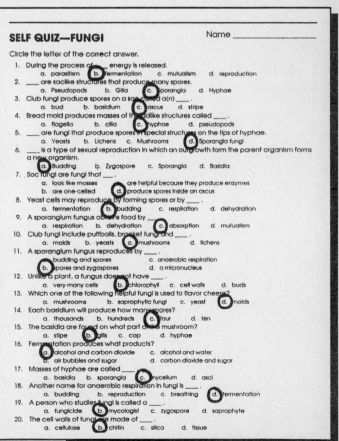

Page 43

SELF QUIZ—FUNGI

Name _____

Circle the letter of the correct answer.

1. During the process of ___ energy is released.
   a. parasitism **b. fermentation** c. mutualism d. reproduction
2. ___ are saclike structures that produce many spores.
   a. Pseudopods b. Gilla **c. Sporangia** d. Hyphae
3. Club fungi produce spores on a sac called a(n) ___.
   a. bud b. basidium **c. ascus** d. stripe
4. Bread mold produces masses of threadlike structures called ___.
   a. flagella b. cilia **c. hyphae** d. pseudopods
5. ___ are fungi that produce spores in special structures on the tips of hyphae.
   a. Yeasts b. Lichens c. Mushrooms **d. Sporangia fungi**
6. ___ is a type of sexual reproduction in which an outgrowth form the parent organism forms a new organism.
   a. Budding b. Zygospore c. Sporangia d. Basidia
7. Sac fungi are fungi that ___.
   a. look like mosses ___ are helpful because they produce enzymes
   b. are one-celled **d.** produce spores inside an ascus
8. Yeast cells may reproduce by forming spores or by ___.
   a. fermentation **b. budding** c. respiration d. dehydration
9. A sporangium fungus obtains food by ___.
   a. respiration b. dehydration **c. absorption** d. mutualism
10. Club fungi include puffballs, bracket fungi and ___.
   a. molds b. yeasts **c. mushrooms** d. lichens
11. A sporangium fungus reproduces by ___.
   ___ budding and spores c. anaerobic respiration
   b. spores and zygospores d. a micronucleus
12. Unlike a plant, a fungus does not have ___.
   a. very many cells **b. chlorophyll** c. cell walls d. buds
13. Which one of the following helpful fungi is used to flavor cheese?
   a. mushrooms b. saprophytic fungi c. yeast **d. molds**
14. Each basidium will produce how many spores?
   a. thousands b. hundreds **c. four** d. ten
15. The basidia are found on what part of the mushroom?
   a. stipe **b. gills** c. cap d. hyphae
16. Fermentation produces what products?
   a. alcohol and carbon dioxide c. alcohol and water
   b. air bubbles and sugar d. carbon dioxide and sugar
17. Masses of hyphae are called ___.
   a. basidia b. sporangia **c. mycelium** d. asci
18. Another name for anaerobic respiration in fungi is ___.
   a. budding b. reproduction c. breathing **d. fermentation**
19. A person who studies fungi is called a ___.
   a. fungicide **b. mycologist** c. zygospore d. saprophyte
20. The cell walls of fungi are made of ___.
   a. cellulose **b. chitin** c. silica d. tissue

Page 44

CROSS-SECTION OF A LEAF

Name _____

Label the following parts of the leaf in the diagram below. Give the purpose/function of each part.

a. lower epidermis—outmost tissue on lower side of leaf

b. upper epidermis—outmost tissue on upper side of leaf

c. palisade layer—rows of elongated cells in upper center of leaf

d. cuticle—waxy substance covering the epidermis

e. stoma—opening between two guard cells on lower side of leaf

f. guard cells—two sausage-shaped cells surrounding each stoma

g. vein (fibrovascular bundle)— supply structural support for leaf and contain xylem and phloem

h. spongy layer—irregular-shaped cells in lower center of leaf

i. air space—space in the spongy layer; contain gases

j. xylem—transports water and minerals to the cells of the leaf

k. phloem—transports sugar and other products of photosynthesis from the leaves to other parts of the plant

l. chloroplasts—cells of a leaf that contain chlorophyll

m. mesophyll—middle tissue of a leaf

Page 45

LEAF CROSSWORD

Name _____

Across

3. outermost cellular layer of the leaf
5. where most photosynthesis takes place in the leaf
8. carry food and water to the cells
10. food-making process occurring in leaves
11. gas necessary for photosynthesis
12. green pigment necessary for photosynthesis

Down

1. control the size of the stoma opening
2. allow the exchange of gases between the environment and the air spaces inside the leaf
4. organelles that contain chlorophyll
6. beneath the palisade layer
7. end product of photosynthesis
9. waxy coat of the leaf

Crossword answers:
- STOMATA
- EPIDERMIS
- GUARDCELLS
- CHLOROPLASTS
- PALISADELAYER
- VEINS
- SPONGYLAYER
- PHOTOSYNTHESIS
- GLUCOSE
- CUTICLE
- CARBONDIOXIDE
- CHLOROPHYLL

Page 46

STRUCTURE OF A ROOT

Name _____

Label the following parts on the diagram below.

a. xylem
b. phloem
c. vascular tissues
d. epidermis
e. foot hair
f. root cap
g. cortex
h. pericycle
i. cambium
j. region of differentiation
k. region of elongation
l. region of meristematic growth

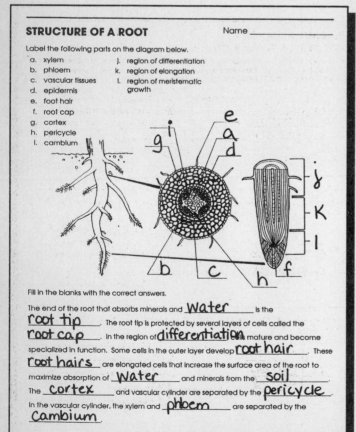

Fill in the blanks with the correct answers.

The end of the root that absorbs minerals and **Water** is the **root tip**. The root tip is protected by several layers of cells called the **root cap**. In the region of **differentiation** mature and become specialized in function. Some cells in the outer layer develop **root hair**. These **root hairs** are elongated cells that increase the surface area of the root to maximize absorption of **Water** and minerals from the **soil**. The **cortex** and vascular cylinder are separated by the **pericycle**. In the vascular cylinder, the xylem and **phloem** are separated by the **Cambium**.

Page 47

STRUCTURE OF A FLOWER

Name _____

Label the parts of the flower in the diagram below. Give the purpose/function of each part.

a. ovary—swollen base of the pistil

b. style—slender, middle portion of a pistil

c. stigma—sticky tip at top of style

d. sepal—leaflike structure that encloses the flower bud

e. receptacle—base of a flower

f. pedicel—stalk on which the flower rests

g. petal—modified, colored leaf of the flower

h. filament—thin, stemlike part of the stamen

i. anther—upper portion of stamen in which pollen is produced

j. pollengrain—spore

k. pistil—female part of a flower

l. stamen—male part of a flower

m. ovule—part of ovary in which eggs are produced

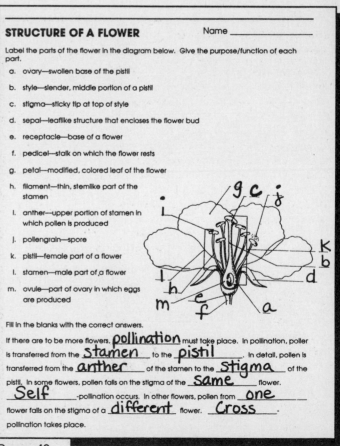

Fill in the blanks with the correct answers.

If there are to be more flowers, **pollination** must take place. In pollination, pollen is transferred from the **stamen** to the **pistil**. In detail, pollen is transferred from the **anther** of the stamen to the **stigma** of the pistil. In some flowers, pollen falls on the stigma of the **same** flower. **Self**-pollination occurs. In other flowers, pollen from **one** flower falls on the stigma of a **different** flower. **Cross**-pollination takes place.

Page 48

ANSWER KEY

STRUCTURE OF THE STAMEN AND A POLLEN GRAIN

Name _____

Label the following parts on the diagrams of double fertilization in the flower below.

a. anther
b. filament
c. pollen grain
d. generative nucleus
e. sperm nuclei
f. tube nucleus
g. pollen tube
h. stigma
i. style
j. ovary
k. ovule
l. embryo sac
m. egg
n. micropyle
o. polar nuclei
p. endosperm nucleus
q. fertilized egg

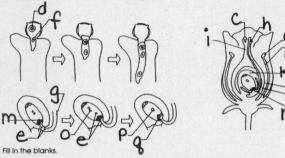

Fill in the blanks.

Each pollen grain contains 2 sperm nuclei, one is a __tube__ nucleus and the other a __generative__ nucleus. After pollination, the pollen grain that falls on the __stigma__ begins to form a __pollen tube__, probably under the control of the __tube__ nucleus. The pollen tube grows through the __style__ into the ovary. The __generative__ nucleus moves down the __pollen tube__ where it divides into __two__ sperm nuclei. Inside the embryo sac, one __sperm__ nucleus joins with the __egg__ nucleus, producing a fertilized __egg__. This is the process of __fertilization__. The second __sperm__ nucleus joins with the __polar__ nuclei to form an __endosperm__ nucleus, which develops into the __endosperm__.

Page 49

METAMORPHOSIS

Name _____

As insects develop they undergo metamorphosis, a series of definite changes in appearance. Some insects, such as a butterfly, undergo complete metamorphosis. Other insects, such as the grasshopper, undergo incomplete metamorphosis.

Label the four stages on the diagram of the complete metamorphosis of the butterfly to the left below.

Label the three stages on the diagram of the incomplete metamorphosis of the grasshopper to the right below.

Complete Metamorphosis   Incomplete Metamorphosis

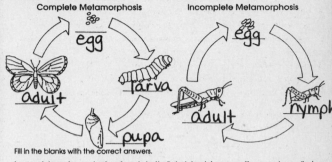

Fill in the blanks with the correct answers.

In complete metamorphosis, a female butterfly hatches into a wormlike organism called a __larva__ or caterpillar. During this stage, the organism consumes a large amount of food. The __larva__ or caterpillar then spins a protective covering around itself and becomes a __pupa__ or chrysalis. This covering is called a __cocoon__. While inside this covering, the __pupa__ changes into an __adult__.

In __incomplete__ metamorphosis, a grasshopper goes through a __gradual__ change from egg to __adult__. The grasshopper begins as an __egg__ and hatches into a __nymph__. A nymph is an immature __grasshopper__ that resembles a full-grown grasshopper but lacks __wings__. As the nymph grows, it __molts__ until it reaches the last stage, the __adult__.

Page 50

STRUCTURE OF A BIRD'S EGG

Name _____

Label the parts of the newly fertilized bird's egg and the developing bird's egg in the diagrams below. State the purpose/function of each part.

a. shell—thick outside covering of the egg

b. amnion—sac surrounding the embryo

c. amniotic fluid—protects embryo from injury and keeps it moist

d. embryo—developing bird

e. chorion—membrane surrounding both embryo and yolk sac

f. yolk sac—contains nutrients for the developing bird

g. blood vessels—lead to yolk sac from the embryo

h. allantois—carries out respiration and receives waste from embryo

i. albumin—white portion of the egg

j. air space—area in flatter end of egg where gases interchange

k. shell membrane—thin layer just inside the shell

l. yolk—source of food for the developing embryo; yellow

m. chalaza—twisted strands that suspend the yolk and developing embryo in egg

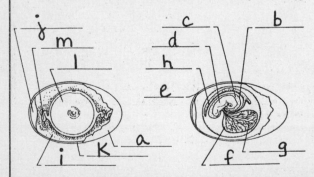

Page 51

PUNNETT SQUARES— CROSSES INVOLVING ONE TRAIT

Name _____

In a certain species of animal, black fur (B) is dominate over brown fur (b). Using the following Punnett square, predict the genotypes and phenotypes of the offspring whose parents are both Bb or have heterozygous black fur.

	B	b
B	BB	Bb
b	Bb	bb

Genotypes: __25__ % homozygous black fur (BB)
__50__ % heterozygous black fur (Bb)
__25__ % homozygous brown fur (bb)

Phenotypes: __75__ % black fur
__25__ % brown fur

Now do the same when one parent is homozygous black and the other is homozygous brown.

	B	B
b	Bb	Bb
b	Bb	Bb

Genotypes: __0__ % homozygous black fur (BB)
__100__ % heterozygous black fur (Bb)
__0__ % homozygous brown fur (bb)

Phenotypes: __100__ % black fur
__0__ % brown fur

Repeat this process again when one parent is heterozygous black and the other is homozygous brown.

	B	b
b	Bb	bb
b	Bb	bb

Genotypes: __0__ % homozygous black fur (BB)
__50__ % heterozygous black fur (Bb)
__50__ % homozygous brown fur (bb)

Phenotypes: __50__ % black fur
__50__ % brown fur

Page 52

BLOOD TYPE AND INHERITANCE

Name _____

In blood typing, the gene for Type A and the gene for Type B are codominant. The gene for type O is recessive. Using Punnett squares, determine the possible blood types of the offspring when:

1. Father is Type O, Mother is Type O

	O	O
O	OO	OO
O	OO	OO

__100__ % O
__0__ % A
__0__ % B
__0__ % AB

2. Father is Type A, homozygous; Mother is Type B, homozygous

	A	A
B	AB	AB
B	AB	AB

__0__ % O
__0__ % A
__0__ % B
__100__ % AB

3. Father is Type A, heterozygous; Mother is Type B, heterozygous

	A	O
B	AB	BO
O	AO	OO

__25__ % O
__25__ % A
__25__ % B
__25__ % AB

4. Father is Type O, Mother is Type AB

	O	O
A	AO	AO
B	BO	BO

__0__ % O
__50__ % A
__50__ % B
__0__ % AB

5. Father and Mother are both Type AB

	A	B
A	AA	AB
B	AB	BB

__0__ % O
__25__ % A
__25__ % B
__50__ % AB

Page 53

PUNNETT SQUARES— CROSSES INVOLVING TWO TRAITS

Name _____

In a dihybrid cross, when two traits are considered, the number of possible combinations in the offspring increases. Suppose that black hair (B) is dominant over blonde hair (b) and brown eyes (E) are dominant over blue eyes (e).

What percent of offspring could be expected to have blonde hair and blue eyes if:

1. The father has black hair (heterozygous) and brown eyes (heterozygous) and the mother has blonde hair and blue eyes.

   Genotype of father—BbEe

   Genotype of mother—bbee

   In the Punnett square below, complete the remaining gametes of the father. Then, fill in the boxes below.

	BE	Be	bE	be
be	BbEe	Bbee	bbEe	bbee
be	BbEe	Bbee	bbEe	bbee
be	BbEe	Bbee	bbEe	bbee
be	BbEe	Bbee	bbEe	bbee

25 %

2. Both parents have black hair (heterozygous) and brown eyes (heterozygous).

   Genotype of father—BbEe

   Genotype of Mother—BbEe

Complete the Punnett square below.

	BE	Be	bE	be
BE	BBEE	BBEe	BbEE	BbEe
Be	BBEe	BBee	BbEe	Bbee
bE	BbEE	BbEe	bbEE	bbEe
be	BbEe	Bbee	bbEe	bbee

6.25 %

In each dihybrid cross, the phenotype ratio of individuals with brown hair and brown eyes, brown hair and blue eyes, blonde hair and brown eyes and blonde hair and blue eyes is 9:3:3:1 .

Page 54

HUMAN PEDIGREES

Name _____

By studying a human pedigree, you can determine whether a trait is dominant or recessive. To interpret the three pedigrees below, use the same key shown to the right. Of course, the individual with the trait could be homozygous dominant or heterozygous dominant.

- ■ male with trait
- □ male without trait
- ● female with trait
- ○ female without trait

A. The pedigree shows the inheritance of attached earlobes for four generations.

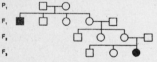

Is the trait for attached earlobes, versus free earlobes, dominant or recessive?

recessive   How do you know?   **If it were dominant it could not show up in F₃ generation unless at least one parent in F₂ generation showed the trait.**

B. The pedigree shows the inheritance of tongue rolling.

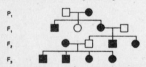

Is this trait dominant or recessive?   **dominant**   Explain.   **The female parent in F₁ generation must be heterozygous dominant, or she could not have two children with the trait.**

C. This pedigree shows the inheritance of colorblindness, a sex-linked trait.

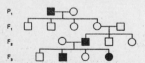

Is this trait dominant or recessive?   **recessive**   Is the mother of the colorblind girl in the F₃ generation colorblind, a carrier, or a person with normal color vision?

carrier   Explain.   **As a young woman needs two genes to be colorblind, her mother must have carried a gene for the trait.**

Page 55

DNA MOLECULE

Name _____

The building blocks of the DNA molecule are nucleotides, which consist of a phosphate, a deoxyribose sugar and a nitrogenous base. In the diagram, label these three substances in the nucleotide at the upper left. The letters representing the four different nitrogenous bases are shown in the nucleotides at the right. Place the name of the base next to its letter symbol in the appropriate space.

A = adenine
T = thymine
G = guanine
C = cytosine

The DNA molecule has a double helix shape. Two strands of DNA are coiled around each other and attached by bonds between the nitrogenous bases of each chain. Adenine always bonds with thymine, and cytosine bonds with guanine.

In the illustration at the left below, label a phosphate and a deoxyribose sugar. Fill in the symbol for each base depending on its complementary base in the opposite strand.

The diagram at the right shows the replication, or duplication, of DNA. Fill in the symbol for each base. Label the original strand, a new strand and a free-floating nucleotide.

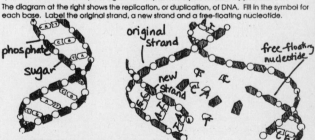

Fill in the blanks with the correct answers.

The structure of DNA was determined by Watson and Crick.

They determined that the DNA molecule was shaped like a double helix. As a result of replication, two identical molecules of DNA are produced. A gene is a sequence of nucleotides in a DNA molecule.

Page 56

ANSWER KEY

mRNA AND TRANSCRIPTION

Name _____

Transcription

Fill in the blanks below. On the illustration of transcription, label the DNA, the newly-forming mRNA and the completed strand of mRNA. Then, fill in the symbol for the correct complementary bases on the newly-forming mRNA molecule.

Messenger RNA (mRNA) carries the instructions to make a particular __protein__ from the DNA in the __nucleus__ to the ribosomes. The process of producing mRNA from instructions in the DNA is called __transcription__

During transcription, the DNA molecule unwinds and separates, exposing the nitrogenous bases. Free RNA __nucleotides__ pair with the exposed bases. There is no __thymine__ (T) in RNA. __Uracil__ (U) pairs with adenine (A) instead. RNA contains the sugar __ribose__ instead of deoxyribose. The mRNA molecule is completed by the formation of __bonds__ between the RNA __nucleotides__, and it then separates from the DNA. The mRNA molecule is a __single__ strand, unlike DNA.

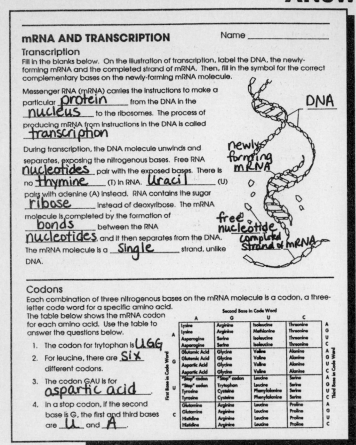

DNA

newly forming mRNA

free nucleotide

completed strand of mRNA

Codons

Each combination of three nitrogenous bases on the mRNA molecule is a codon, a three-letter code word for a specific amino acid. The table below shows the mRNA codon for each amino acid. Use the table to answer the questions below.

1. The codon for trytophan is __UGG__

2. For leucine, there are __six__ different codons.

3. The codon GAU is for __aspartic acid__

4. In a stop codon, if the second base is G, the first and third bases are __U__ and __A__.

Second Base in Code Word

	A	G	U	C
A	Lysine / Lysine / Asparagine / Asparagine	Arginine / Arginine / Serine / Serine	Isoleucine / Methionine / Isoleucine / Isoleucine	Threonine / Threonine / Threonine / Threonine
G	Glutamic Acid / Glutamic Acid / Aspartic Acid / Aspartic Acid	Glycine / Glycine / Glycine / Glycine	Valine / Valine / Valine / Valine	Alanine / Alanine / Alanine / Alanine
U	*Stop* codon / *Stop* codon / Tyrosine / Tyrosine	*Stop* codon / Trytophan / Cysteine / Cysteine	Leucine / Leucine / Phenylalanine / Phenylalanine	Serine / Serine / Serine / Serine
C	Glutamine / Glutamine / Histidine / Histidine	Arginine / Arginine / Arginine / Arginine	Leucine / Leucine / Leucine / Leucine	Proline / Proline / Proline / Proline

---

GENETICS CROSSWORD

Name _____

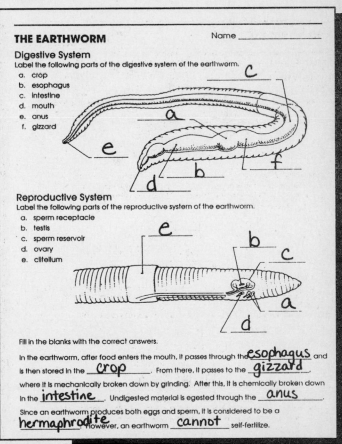

Crossword answers:
- TRANSLOCATION
- DIHYBRID
- CHROMOSOMES
- DOMINANCE
- PUNNETTSQUARE
- URACIL
- GENOTYPE
- TRANSLATION
- GENES
- ALLELE
- RIBOSE
- TRANSCRIPTION
- DEOXYRIBOSE

Across

1. Occurs when a segment of chromosome breaks off and becomes reattached to another chromosome
4. An organism that is heterozygous for two traits
7. Humans have 46 of these.
8. Capacity of one allele to suppress the expression of a contrasting, recessive gene
10. Diagram used to predict the results of genetic crosses
11. This base is found in RNA, but not in DNA
12. Genetic makeup of an individual
16. Assembly of a protein molecule according to the code in a mRNA molecule
17. The sugar in RNA
18. Found on chromosomes, they determine specific characteristics of the organism
19. Different form of a gene
20. The process of producing mRNA from instructions in DNA
21. Sugar in DNA

Down

2. Occurs when both alleles are equally dominant
3. Subunit of DNA consisting of a nitrogenous base, a sugar and a phosphate group
5. Double helix in which the genetic code is found
6. Two dominant or two recessive genes for the same trait
9. Process by which DNA makes an exact copy of itself
10. Appearance of an individual due to its genetic makeup
13. Presence of complete extra sets of chromosomes
14. Conducted experiments on heredity in pea plants
15. Site of protein synthesis

UROGENITAL SYSTEM OF A FROG

Name _____

Label the following parts of the urinary and reproductive systems of a female frog.

a. fat bodies
b. oviduct
c. egg mass
d. adrenal gland
e. ureter
f. uteri
g. kidney
h. cloaca
i. urinary bladder

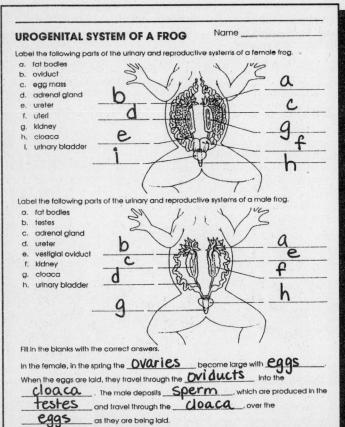

Label the following parts of the urinary and reproductive systems of a male frog.

a. fat bodies
b. testis
c. adrenal gland
d. ureter
e. vestigial oviduct
f. kidney
g. cloaca
h. urinary bladder

Fill in the blanks with the correct answers.

In the female, in the spring the __ovaries__ become large with __eggs__ When the eggs are laid, they travel through the __oviducts__ into the __cloaca__. The male deposits __sperm__, which are produced in the __testes__ and travel through the __cloaca__, over the __eggs__ as they are being laid.

THE EARTHWORM

Name _____

Digestive System

Label the following parts of the digestive system of the earthworm.

a. crop
b. esophagus
c. intestine
d. mouth
e. anus
f. gizzard

Reproductive System

Label the following parts of the reproductive system of the earthworm.

a. sperm receptacle
b. testis
c. sperm reservoir
d. ovary
e. clitellum

Fill in the blanks with the correct answers.

In the earthworm, after food enters the mouth, it passes through the __esophagus__ and is then stored in the __crop__. From there, it passes to the __gizzard__, where it is mechanically broken down by grinding. After this, it is chemically broken down in the __intestine__. Undigested material is egested through the __anus__.

Since an earthworm produces both eggs and sperm, it is considered to be a __hermaphrodite__. However, an earthworm __cannot__ self-fertilize.

ANSWER KEY

THE GRASSHOPPER

Name _____

External Anatomy
Label the following parts of the external anatomy of the grasshopper.

a. antenna
b. simple eye
c. compound eye
d. ear
e. legs
f. wings
g. egg-laying apparatus
h. spiracles

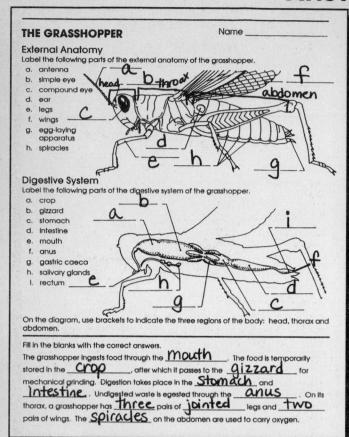

Digestive System
Label the following parts of the digestive system of the grasshopper.

a. crop
b. gizzard
c. stomach
d. intestine
e. mouth
f. anus
g. gastric caeca
h. salivary glands
i. rectum

On the diagram, use brackets to indicate the three regions of the body: head, thorax and abdomen.

Fill in the blanks with the correct answers.

The grasshopper ingests food through the **mouth**. The food is temporarily stored in the **crop**, after which it passes to the **gizzard** for mechanical grinding. Digestion takes place in the **stomach** and **Intestine**. Undigested waste is egested through the **anus**. On its thorax, a grasshopper has **three** pairs of **jointed** legs and **two** pairs of wings. The **spiracles** on the abdomen are used to carry oxygen.

THE FROG—PART I

Name _____

Digestive System
Label the following parts of the digestive system of a frog.

a. mouth
b. esophagus
c. liver
d. gall bladder
e. pancreas
f. stomach
g. small intestine
h. large intestine
i. cloaca
j. anus

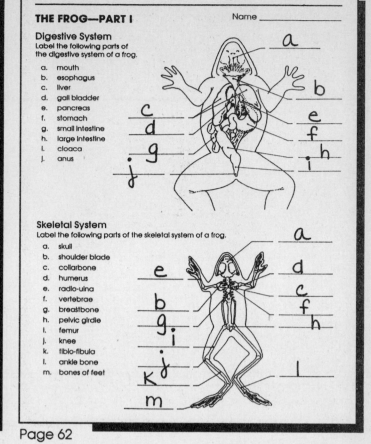

Skeletal System
Label the following parts of the skeletal system of a frog.

a. skull
b. shoulder blade
c. collarbone
d. humerus
e. radio-ulna
f. vertebrae
g. breastbone
h. pelvic girdle
i. femur
j. knee
k. tibia-fibula
l. ankle bone
m. bones of feet

CIRCULATORY SYSTEMS

Name _____

Label the following parts of the circulatory system of the earthworm in the diagram.

a. aortic arches
b. ventral blood vessel
c. dorsal blood vessel

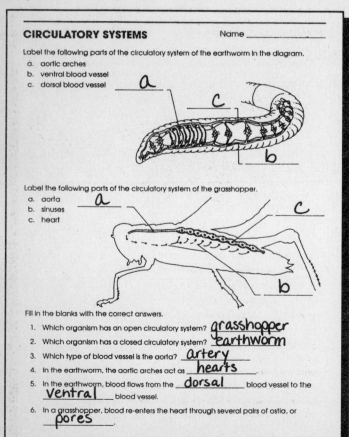

Label the following parts of the circulatory system of the grasshopper.

a. aorta
b. sinuses
c. heart

Fill in the blanks with the correct answers.

1. Which organism has an open circulatory system? **grasshopper**
2. Which organism has a closed circulatory system? **earthworm**
3. Which type of blood vessel is the aorta? **artery**
4. In the earthworm, the aortic arches act as **hearts**
5. In the earthworm, blood flows from the **dorsal** blood vessel to the **ventral** blood vessel.
6. In a grasshopper, blood re-enters the heart through several pairs of ostia, or **pores**.

GAS EXCHANGE IN LIVING ORGANISMS

Name _____

Fill in the blanks with the correct answers.

1. In the simplest organisms, where the outer membrane of the organism is in direct contact with the environment, the exchange of gases occurs by the process of **diffusion**.
2. In plants, the exchange of gases occur mainly through the **roots** and **leaves**
3. In the hydra, gas exchange occurs directly between the water and the cells through the process of **diffusion**.
4. In the earthworm, the exchange of gases occurs through the **skin**.
5. Label the following parts of the respiratory system of the grasshopper on the diagram.

   a. air sacs
   b. tracheal tubes
   c. spiracles

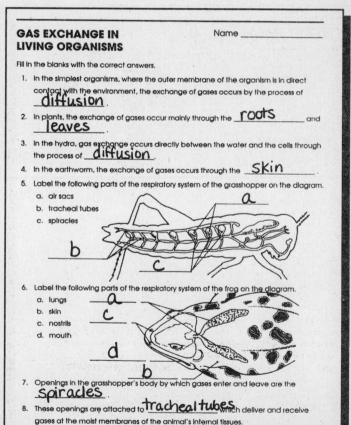

6. Label the following parts of the respiratory system of the frog on the diagram.

   a. lungs
   b. skin
   c. nostrils
   d. mouth

7. Openings in the grasshopper's body by which gases enter and leave are the **spiracles**.
8. These openings are attached to **tracheal tubes** which deliver and receive gases at the moist membranes of the animal's internal tissues.

ANSWER KEY

EXCRETION IN LIVING ORGANISMS

Name _____

Fill in the blanks with the correct answers.

1. In one-celled organisms and plants, excess water or toxic substances can be contained in **vacuoles**. Specialized types of these organelles, called **contractile vacuoles**, can expel these substances from the cell.

2. In the hydra, metabolic waste products are discharged directly into the **water**. Gases are also exchanged between the cells and the **water**.

3. Label the following parts of the excretory system of the earthworm on the diagram.
   a. nephridium
   b. excretory pore
   c. tubule

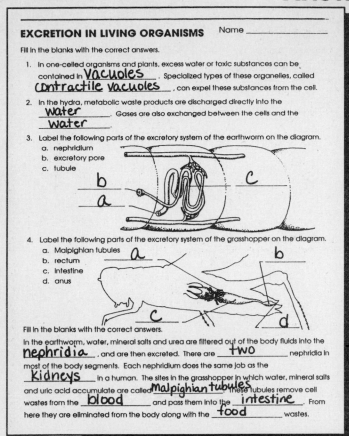

4. Label the following parts of the excretory system of the grasshopper on the diagram.
   a. Malpighian tubules
   b. rectum
   c. intestine
   d. anus

Fill in the blanks with the correct answers.

In the earthworm, water, mineral salts and urea are filtered out of the body fluids into the **nephridia**, and are then excreted. There are **two** nephridia in most of the body segments. Each nephridium does the same job as the **kidneys** in a human. The sites in the grasshopper in which water, mineral salts and uric acid accumulate are called **Malpighian tubules**. These tubules remove cell wastes from the **blood** and pass them into the **intestine**. From here they are eliminated from the body along with the **food** wastes.

NERVOUS SYSTEMS OF THE EARTHWORM AND GRASSHOPPER

Name _____

Label the following parts of the nervous system of the earthworm on the diagram below.
a. brain
b. nerves
c. ventral nerve cord
d. ganglia

Label the following parts of the nervous system of the grasshopper on the diagram below.
a. brain
b. antennae
c. compound eye
d. nerves
e. ventral nerve cord
f. ganglia

Fill in the blanks with the correct answers.

In the earthworm, two nerves from the paired **brain** run around each side of the **pharynx** to the **ventral** side of the worm. Here they join to become a double **nerve** cord which runs to the last segment. In each **segment**, they join to become an enlarged **ganglion**.

In the grasshopper, the most prominent parts of the brain are the **optic** lobes. The large **compound** eyes are made up of many **lenses** so the grasshopper can see in many directions at the same time. The **ventral** nerve cord contains many **ganglia**. The largest ganglion sends messages to the **jumping** legs.

THE FROG—PART II

Name _____

Nervous System

Label the following parts of the nervous system of a frog.
a. olfactory lobe
b. cerebrum
c. optic lobe
d. cerebellum
e. medulla oblongata
f. cranial nerves
g. spinal cord
h. spinal nerves
i. brachial nerve
j. sciatic nerve
k. chain of autonomic ganglia

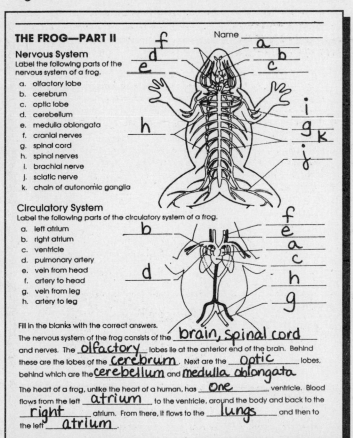

Circulatory System

Label the following parts of the circulatory system of a frog.
a. left atrium
b. right atrium
c. ventricle
d. pulmonary artery
e. vein from head
f. artery to head
g. vein from leg
h. artery to leg

Fill in the blanks with the correct answers.

The nervous system of the frog consists of the **brain, spinal cord** and nerves. The **olfactory** lobes lie at the anterior end of the brain. Behind these are the lobes of the **cerebrum**. Next are the **optic** lobes, behind which are the **cerebellum** and **medulla oblongata**.

The heart of a frog, unlike the heart of a human, has **one** ventricle. Blood flows from the left **atrium** to the ventricle, around the body and back to the **right** atrium. From there, it flows to the **lungs** and then to the left **atrium**.

STRUCTURE OF A STARFISH

Name _____

Label the following parts of a starfish on the diagram below. Give the purpose/function of each part.

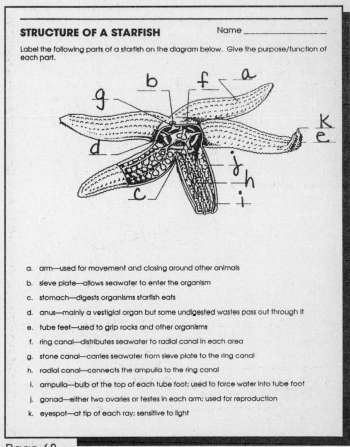

a. arm—used for movement and closing around other animals

b. sieve plate—allows seawater to enter the organism

c. stomach—digests organisms starfish eats

d. anus—mainly a vestigial organ but some undigested wastes pass out through it

e. tube feet—used to grip rocks and other organisms

f. ring canal—distributes seawater to radial canal in each area

g. stone canal—carries seawater from sieve plate to the ring canal

h. radial canal—connects the ampulla to the ring canal

i. ampulla—bulb at the top of each tube foot; used to force water into tube foot

j. gonad—either two ovaries or testes in each arm; used for reproduction

k. eyespot—at tip of each ray; sensitive to light

ANSWER KEY

STRUCTURE OF A CRAYFISH

Name _____

Label the following parts of the crayfish on the diagrams of the dorsal and/or ventral views below.

a. carapace
b. compound eye
c. antennule
d. mandible
e. cheliped
f. antenna
g. walking legs
h. swimmerets
i. uropod
j. telson
k. anus
l. cephalothorax
m. abdomen

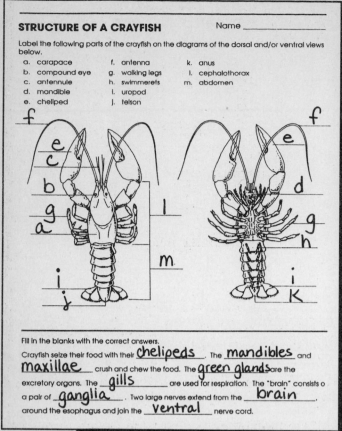

Fill in the blanks with the correct answers.

Crayfish seize their food with their **chelipeds**. The **mandibles** and **maxillae** crush and chew the food. The **green glands** are the excretory organs. The **gills** are used for respiration. The "brain" consists o a pair of **ganglia**. Two large nerves extend from the **brain**, around the esophagus and join the **ventral** nerve cord.

STRUCTURE OF A BONY FISH

Name _____

Label the following parts of a fish on the diagrams below of the external and/or internal structure.

a. gills
b. brain
c. spinal cord
d. swimbladder
e. dorsal fins
f. caudal fin
g. anal fin
h. lateral line
i. operculum
j. gill filaments
k. mouth
l. intestine
m. pelvic fin
n. liver
o. stomach
p. heart
q. kidney
r. gall bladder
s. urinary bladder
t. urogenital opening
u. anus
v. ovary/testis
w. pyloric caeca
x. pectoral fin
y. eyes

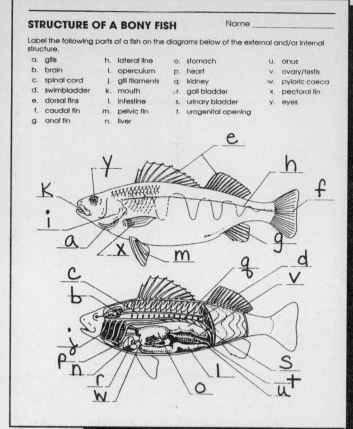

INTERNAL STRUCTURE OF A BIRD

Name _____

Label the following parts of the internal structure of a bird on the diagram below.

a. ureter
b. crop
c. heart
d. liver
e. lung
f. trachea
g. kidney
h. cloaca
i. esophagus
j. intestine
k. gall bladder
l. gizzard

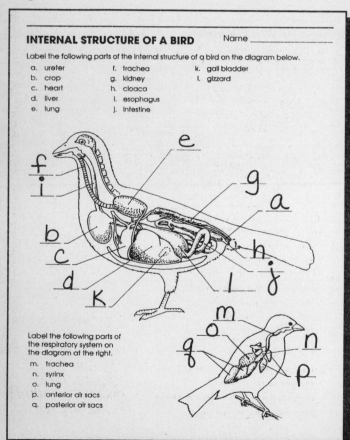

Label the following parts of the respiratory system on the diagram at the right.

m. trachea
n. syrinx
o. lung
p. anterior air sacs
q. posterior air sacs

THE HUMAN DIGESTIVE SYSTEM

Name _____

Label the following parts of the human digestive system on the diagram below.

a. mouth
b. salivary glands
c. esophagus
d. stomach
e. liver
f. pancreas
g. small intestine
h. large intestine
i. rectum
j. anus
k. appendix
l. gall bladder

Accessory Organs
Food does not pass through three organs in the digestive system. Label the three accessory organs in the diagram to the right.

m. liver
n. gall bladder
o. pancreas

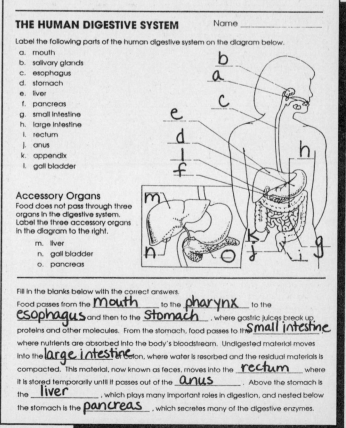

Fill in the blanks below with the correct answers.

Food passes from the **mouth** to the **pharynx** to the **esophagus** and then to the **stomach**, where gastric juices break up proteins and other molecules. From the stomach, food passes to the **small intestine** where nutrients are absorbed into the body's bloodstream. Undigested material moves into the **large intestine** or colon, where water is resorbed and the residual materials is compacted. This material, now known as feces, moves into the **rectum** where it is stored temporarily until it passes out of the **anus**. Above the stomach is the **liver**, which plays many important roles in digestion, and nested below the stomach is the **pancreas**, which secretes many of the digestive enzymes.

ANSWER KEY

THE MOUTH AND TEETH

Name _____

Label the following parts of the tooth on the diagram below.

a. gum
b. nerves and blood vessels
c. dentin
d. enamel
e. pulp
f. crown
g. neck
h. root
i. cementum
j. bone

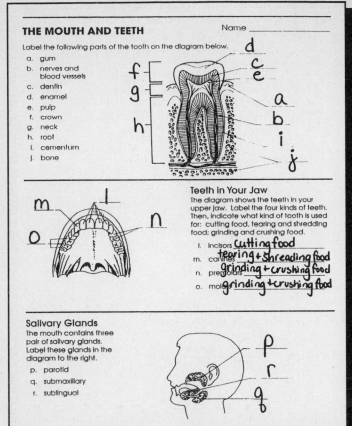

Teeth in Your Jaw

The diagram shows the teeth in your upper jaw. Label the four kinds of teeth. Then, indicate what kind of tooth is used for: cutting food, tearing and shredding food; grinding and crushing food.

l. incisors — cutting food
m. canines — tearing + shredding food
n. premolars — grinding + crushing food
o. molars — grinding + crushing food

Salivary Glands

The mouth contains three pair of salivary glands. Label these glands in the diagram to the right.

p. parotid
q. submaxillary
r. sublingual

Page 73

HUMAN DIGESTIVE SYSTEM CROSSWORD

Name _____

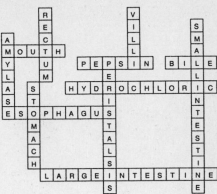

Across

5. Chemical digestion of carbohydrates begins here.
6. Enzyme that begins the digestion of proteins
8. Produced by the liver, this emulsifies fats to make digestion easier.
10. Acid present in the stomach
11. Tube between the mouth and stomach
12. Water and certain vitamins are absorbed here from the undigested food.

Down

1. Wastes are stored here before expulsion
2. Fingerlike projections which increase the surface area of the small intestine
3. Long, convoluted tube where chemical digestion is completed
4. Enzyme present in saliva
7. Involuntary muscle contraction that move the food through the digestive system
9. In this muscular pouch, food is mixed with gastric juice.

Page 74

STRUCTURE OF THE HEART

Name _____

Label the following parts of the human heart on the diagram below.

a. aorta
b. left pulmonary artery
c. left pulmonary vein
d. left atrium
e. bicuspid valve (mitral valve)
f. left ventricle
g. septum
h. right ventricle
i. inferior vena cava
j. semilunar valves
k. tricuspid valve
l. right atrium
m. right pulmonary vein
n. right pulmonary artery
o. superior vena cava

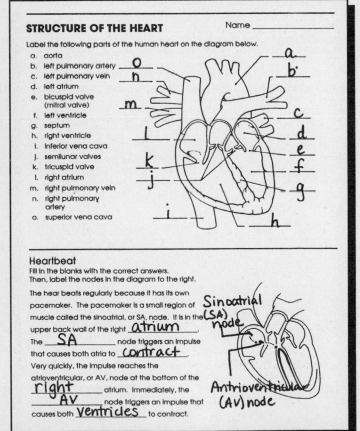

Heartbeat

Fill in the blanks with the correct answers. Then, label the nodes in the diagram to the right.

The hear beats regularly because it has its own pacemaker. The pacemaker is a small region of muscle called the sinoatrial, or SA, node. It is in the upper back wall of the right __atrium__. The __SA__ node triggers an impulse that causes both atria to __contract__. Very quickly, the impulse reaches the atrioventricular, or AV, node at the bottom of the __right__ atrium. Immediately, the __AV__ node triggers an impulse that causes both __ventricles__ to contract.

Sinoatrial (SA) node

Antrioventricular (AV) node

Page 75

HUMAN CIRCULATORY SYSTEM

Name _____

Starting from and ending with the right atrium, trace the flow of blood through the heart and body by numbering the following in the correct order.

1,11	right atrium	4	lungs
6	left atrium	2	right ventricle
3	pulmonary artery	7	left ventricle
10	vena cava	9	body cells
8	aorta	5	pulmonary veins

Starting from and ending with the heart, trace the blood flow through the human circulatory system by numbering the following in the correct order.

1,7	heart	4	capillaries
6	veins	2	arteries
3	arterioles	5	venules

What term best fits each of the following descriptions?

1. vessels which carry blood away fro the heart — arteries
2. vessels which carry blood toward the heart — veins
3. tiny blood vessels with walls that are only one cell thick — capillaries
4. thick wall that divides the heart into two sides — septum
5. upper chambers of the heart that receive blood — atria
6. lower chambers of the heart that pump blood out of the heart — ventricles
7. valve between right atrium and right ventricle — tricuspid
8. valve between left atrium and left ventricle — mitral (bicuspid)
9. valves found between the ventricles and blood vessels — semilunar
10. membrane around the heart — pericardium
11. the only artery in the body rich in carbon dioxide — pulmonary artery
12. the only vein in the body rich in oxygen — pulmonary vein

Page 76

Biology IF8765   121   ©Instructional Fair, Inc.

ANSWER KEY

THE BLOOD
Name _____

Label the following parts on the diagram below.
a. white blood cell
b. red blood cell
c. platelet

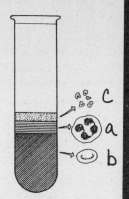

Answer the questions below.

1. What is the role of platelets?—Within a few seconds after an injury, platelets (cell fragments) begin the process of blood clotting.

2. What are sickle cells?—Red blood cells that are crescent-shaped instead of round and concave.

3. Why are they important?—They may clog small blood vessels, depriving tissues of oxygen and causing great pain—even death.

Match the description in Column I with the correct term in Column II.

	Column I		Column II
a)	iron containing molecule in red blood cells	c	plasma
b)	white blood cells which produce antibodies	e	platelets
c)	liquid part of the blood	b	lymphocytes
d)	returns tissue fluid to the blood	f	antigens
e)	cell fragments involved in clotting	i	fibrin
f)	foreign molecules in the body	a	hemoglobin
g)	cancer of the bone marrow	j	antibodies
h)	condition in which the blood cannot carry sufficient oxygen	h	anemia
i)	strands of protein involved in clotting	g	leukemia
j)	react with antigens and inactivates them	d	lymphatic system

Page 77

BLOOD TYPES AND TRANSFUSIONS
Name _____

Fill in the blanks on the table below. Then answer the questions.

Blood Type	Antigens on Red Cells	Antibodies in Plasma	May Donate To	May Receive From
A	A	anti-B	A, AB	A, O
B	B	anti-A	B, AB	B, O
AB	A, B	none	AB	A, B, AB, O
O	none	anti-A anti-B	A, B, AB, O	O

1. Why are individuals with blood type O considered universal donors? People with any blood group may receive type O blood.

2. Why are individuals with blood type AB considered universal recipients? They may receive types A, B, AB and O blood.

3. Today, some people who know they must undergo surgery in the near future give their own blood at the blood bank earlier. Then, they use it during surgery. Why? Today the blood supply is quite safe, but some people are still concerned about blood that could carry the HIV virus

The distribution of blood types around the world varies. For example, you would find it different in Japan, and among Basque people in northern Spain.

POPULATION	A	B	AB	O
U.S. Whites	39.7%	10.6%	3.4%	46.3%
U.S. Blacks	26.5%	20.1%	4.3%	49.1%
Native Americans	30.6%	0.2%	0.00%	69.1%

On the basis of the table, answer the following questions.

1. In the U.S., what is the most frequent blood type? O

2. If you are an African American, what are the chances that your blood is type A? 26.5%

3. What is the only population that has no representative with one blood type? Native Americans

4. What blood type is this? AB

5. Compare the frequency of type B blood between white and black Americans. It is almost twice as frequent among black Americans.

Page 78

THE HUMAN RESPIRATORY SYSTEM
Name _____

Respiratory System
Label the following parts of the human respiratory system on the diagram.
a. nasal passage
b. nostrils
c. mouth
d. epiglottis
e. larynx
f. trachea
g. bronchi
h. bronchiole
i. alveoli
j. diaphragm
k. lung
l. pharynx
m. pleura

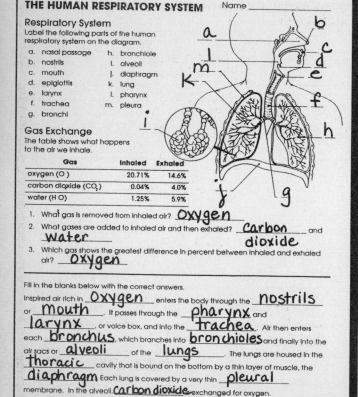

Gas Exchange
The table shows what happens to the air we inhale.

Gas	Inhaled	Exhaled
oxygen (O)	20.71%	14.6%
carbon dioxide (CO₂)	0.04%	4.0%
water (H O)	1.25%	5.9%

1. What gas is removed from inhaled air? Oxygen

2. What gases are added to inhaled air and then exhaled? Carbon and water dioxide

3. Which gas shows the greatest difference in percent between inhaled and exhaled air? Oxygen

Fill in the blanks below with the correct answers.

Inspired air rich in Oxygen enters the body through the nostrils or mouth. It passes through the pharynx and larynx, or voice box, and into the trachea. Air then enters each bronchus, which branches into bronchioles and finally into the air sacs or alveoli of the lungs. The lungs are housed in the thoracic cavity that is bound on the bottom by a thin layer of muscle, the diaphragm. Each lung is covered by a very thin pleural membrane. In the alveoli, carbon dioxide is exchanged for oxygen.

Page 79

HUMAN RESPIRATORY SYSTEM CROSSWORD
Name _____

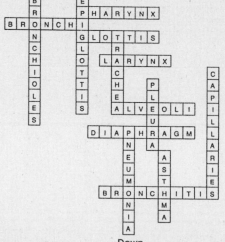

Across
3. Area at the back of the throat where the mouth and nasal cavity meet
4. The trachea divides into these right and left branches
5. Opening to the windpipe
7. Contains the vocal cords
10. Tiny air sacs where the exchange of gases between air and blood takes place
11. Flat sheet of muscle separating the chest cavity from the abdominal cavity
14. Inflammation of the lining of the bronchial tubes

Down
1. Smaller branches of the bronchi
2. Flap of tissue which prevents food from entering windpipe during swallowing
6. Tube leading from larynx to bronchi
8. blood vessels surrounding the air sacs
9. Moist membrane covering the lung and chest cavity wall on each side
12. Infection of the lungs caused by viruses, bacteria or fungi
13. Bronchial spasm resulting in decreased air movement and air trapped in alveoli

Page 80

ANSWER KEY

HUMAN SKIN

Name _____

Label the following parts of human skin on the diagram below.

a. pore
b. hair
c. nerve ending
d. fat cells
e. capillary
f. sweat gland
g. hair follicle
h. epidermis
i. dermis
j. erector muscle
k. subcutaneous tissue

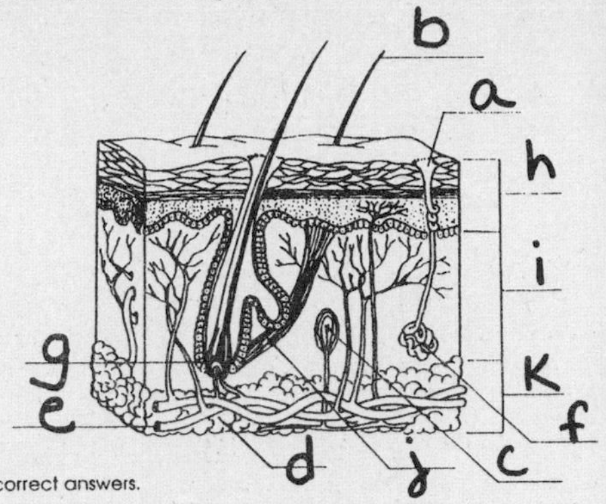

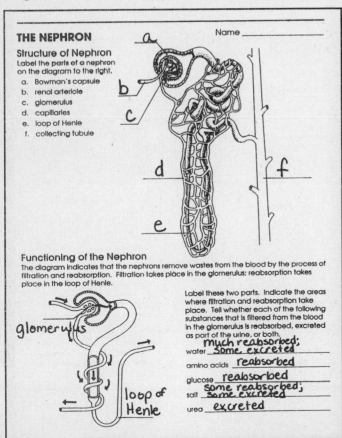

Fill in the blanks with the correct answers.

__Epithelium__ makes up the skin of the body and the lining of the respiratory and digestive tracts. __Skin__ is the largest organ of the vertebrate body, composing 15% of the actual weight in an adult. Vertebrate skin is composed of two layers: the outer __epidermis__ and the lower __dermis__. There is a protective underlying layer, or __subcutaneous__ layer. Cells are constantly lost from the __epidermis__ and replaced by new cells produced deep within the epidermis. It takes about 27 days for all of the outer skin cells to be __replaced__. Specialized cells called melanocytes within the epidermis produce a brownish pigment called __melanin__. People of all races have about the same number of melanocytes but differ in the amount of __melanin__ produced, thus giving a vast range of skin tones. The dermis is composed mainly of __connective__ tissue, which gives the skin its strength and elasticity. Among the structures in the dermis are blood __vessels__, nerves, hair __roots__, oil __glands__ and __sweat__ glands. Wrinkling of the skin occurs in the __dermis__ layer. Leather goods are made of animal __dermis__.

Page 81

HUMAN URINARY TRACT AND KIDNEY

Name _____

Label the parts of the human urinary system, including the human kidney, in the diagram below. Give the function/purpose of each part.

a. kidneys—remove liquids and other substances from blood

b. adrenal glands—produce hormones

c. ureter—joins kidney to bladder

d. urinary bladder—stores urine until released from the body

e. urethra—neck of bladder

f. renal artery—artery leading to the kidneys

g. renal vein—vein going away from the kidneys

h. cortex—outer portion of kidney

i. medulla—inner portion of kidney

j. renal pelvis—central area of kidney

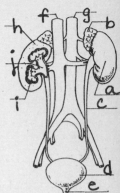

Fill in the blanks below with the correct answers.

Kidneys are the "filters" of the __excretory__ system. They control essential balance between body salts and __water__. They remove from the blood nitrogenous wastes, water, urea, nonvolatile foreign substances, excess salt and excess water. The kidney is enclosed by a connective tissue __capsule__ and is divided into an outer __cortex__ and an inner __medulla__. The __loop of Henle__ functions chiefly for water resorption. The liquid waste, __urine__, collected by the kidneys passes through the __ureter__ to the __urinary bladder__. The urinary bladder is a strong muscular organ that stores the urine until it can be excreted via the __urethra__.

Page 82

THE NEPHRON

Name _____

Structure of Nephron
Label the parts of a nephron on the diagram to the right.

a. Bowman's capsule
b. renal arteriole
c. glomerulus
d. capillaries
e. loop of Henle
f. collecting tubule

Functioning of the Nephron
The diagram indicates that the nephrons remove wastes from the blood by the process of filtration and reabsorption. Filtration takes place in the glomerulus; reabsorption takes place in the loop of Henle.

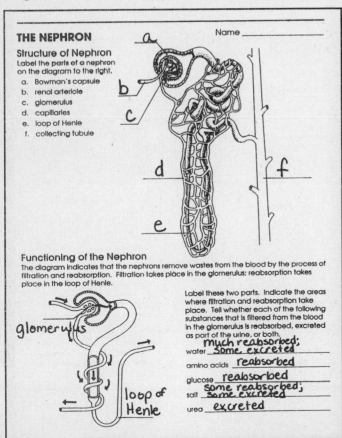

Label these two parts. Indicate the areas where filtration and reabsorption take place. Tell whether each of the following substances that is filtered from the blood in the glomerulus is reabsorbed, excreted as part of the urine, or both.

water __much reabsorbed; some excreted__

amino acids __reabsorbed__

glucose __reabsorbed__

salt __some reabsorbed; some excreted__

urea __excreted__

Page 83

HUMAN EXCRETORY SYSTEM CROSSWORD

Name _____

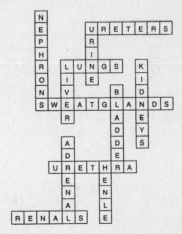

Across
2. Tubes connecting the kidneys to the urinary bladder
3. Carbon dioxide and water are excreted here during exhalation
6. Structures in the skin which excrete water, salts and some urea
8. Urine is expelled from the body through this tube
10. Arteries and veins to kidneys

Down
1. Microscopic units that filter the blood in the kidneys
2. Liquid waste collected and excreted by the kidneys
3. Removes toxic substances from the blood and converts excess amino acids to urea
4. Organs that filter wastes and other dissolved substances out of the blood
5. The urinary ____ stores the urine until it can be excreted by the body.
7. Endocrine gland at the top of each kidney
9. Loop of ____ at the bottom of nephron

Page 84

ANSWER KEY

THE HUMAN SKELETAL SYSTEM

Name _____

Label the following parts of the human skeletal system on the diagram.

a. skull
b. cranium
c. mandible
d. clavicle
e. pectoral girdle
f. scapula
g. sternum
h. ribs
i. humerus
j. vertebrae
k. vertebral column
l. pelvic girdle
m. radius
n. ulna
o. carpals
p. metacarpals
q. phalanges
(on both hands and feet)
r. femur
s. patella
t. tibia
u. fibula
v. tarsals
w. metatarsals

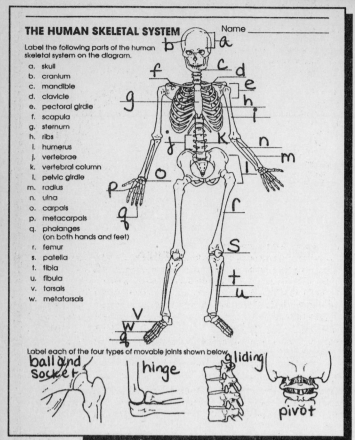

Label each of the four types of movable joints shown below.

ball and socket   hinge   gliding   pivot

STRUCTURE OF BONES

Name _____

Label the following parts of a long bone on both diagrams wherever possible. The diagram at the right shows a longitudinal section, the other a cross section.

a. shaft
b. periosteum
c. blood vessels
d. compact bone
e. spongy bone
f. red marrow
g. nerve cells
h. lamella
i. Haversian canal
j. bone cell

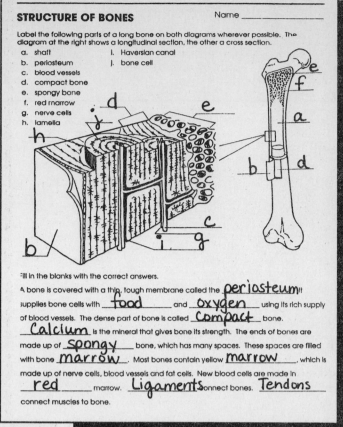

Fill in the blanks with the correct answers.

A bone is covered with a thin, tough membrane called the **periosteum**. It supplies bone cells with **food** and **oxygen** using its rich supply of blood vessels. The dense part of bone is called **compact** bone. **Calcium** is the mineral that gives bone its strength. The ends of bones are made up of **spongy** bone, which has many spaces. These spaces are filled with bone **marrow**. Most bones contain yellow **marrow**, which is made up of nerve cells, blood vessels and fat cells. New blood cells are made in **red** marrow. **Ligaments** connect bones. **Tendons** connect muscles to bone.

NEURON AND NEUROMUSCULAR JUNCTION

Name _____

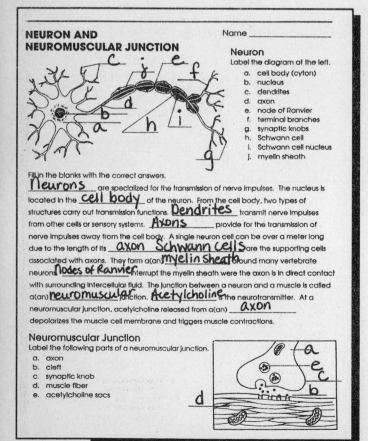

Neuron

Label the diagram at the left.

a. cell body (cyton)
b. nucleus
c. dendrites
d. axon
e. node of Ranvier
f. terminal branches
g. synaptic knobs
h. Schwann cell
i. Schwann cell nucleus
j. myelin sheath

Fill in the blanks with the correct answers.

Neurons are specialized for the transmission of nerve impulses. The nucleus is located in the **cell body** of the neuron. From the cell body, two types of structures carry out transmission functions. **Dendrites** transmit nerve impulses from other cells or sensory systems. **Axons** provide for the transmission of nerve impulses away from the cell body. A single neuron cell can be over a meter long due to the length of its **axon**. **Schwann cells** are the supporting cells associated with axons. They form a(an) **myelin sheath** around many vertebrate neurons. **Nodes of Ranvier** interrupt the myelin sheath were the axon is in direct contact with surrounding intercellular fluid. The junction between a neuron and a muscle is called a(an) **neuromuscular** junction. **Acetylcholine** is the neurotransmitter. At a neuromuscular junction, acetylcholine released from a(an) **axon** depolarizes the muscle cell membrane and triggers muscle contractions.

Neuromuscular Junction

Label the following parts of a neuromuscular junction.

a. axon
b. cleft
c. synaptic knob
d. muscle fiber
e. acetylcholine sacs

SPINAL CORD AND REFLEX ACT

Name _____

Cross Section of Spinal Cord

Label the following parts of a spinal cord on the cross-section diagram.

a. white matter
b. grey matter
c. dorsal root ganglion
d. nerve fibers
e. interneuron
f. synapse
g. sensory neuron
h. motor neuron

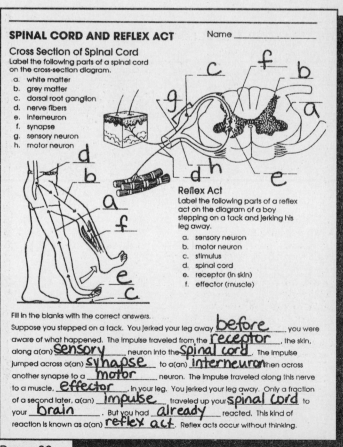

Reflex Act

Label the following parts of a reflex act on the diagram of a boy stepping on a tack and jerking his leg away.

a. sensory neuron
b. motor neuron
c. stimulus
d. spinal cord
e. receptor (in skin)
f. effector (muscle)

Fill in the blanks with the correct answers.

Suppose you stepped on a tack. You jerked your leg away **before** you were aware of what happened. The impulse traveled from the **receptor**, the skin, along to a(an) **sensory** neuron into the **spinal cord**. The impulse jumped across a(an) **synapse** to a(an) **interneuron** then across another synapse to a **motor** neuron. The impulse traveled along this nerve to a muscle. **effector** in your leg. You jerked your leg away. Only a fraction of a second later, a(an) **impulse** traveled up your **spinal cord** to your **brain**. But you had **already** reacted. This kind of reaction is known as a(an) **reflex act**. Reflex acts occur without thinking.

ANSWER KEY

STRUCTURE OF THE BRAIN
Name _____

Label the correct parts of the brain and spinal cord on the diagram at the left below. Give the purpose/function of each part.

a. cerebellum—coordinates balance and action of muscles
b. medulla oblongata—controls breathing, heart rate, blood pressure
c. thalamus—switching station for sensory input
d. hypothalamus—controls secretions of pituitary gland
e. corpus callosum—thick band of fibers joining the cerebral hemispheres
f. pons—provides link between cerebral cortex and cerebellum
g. spinal cord—main nerves of central nervous system extending down from the brain
h. cerebrum—largest part of brain; responsible for voluntary activities
i. pituitary gland—endocrine gland that secretes numerous hormones

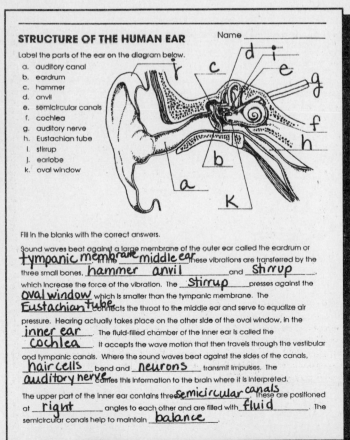

Lobes of the Cerebrum
The diagram to the right above shows the four major lobes of each hemisphere of the cerebrum: frontal, parietal, occipital and temporal. Label each lobe. Then, fill in the blanks below with the correct answers.

The _frontal_ lobes control some body movements, reasoning, judgment and emotions. The sense of vision is located in the _occipital_ lobe. The sense of hearing is interpreted in the _temporal_ lobes. The _parietal_ lobes interpret sensations such as pain, pressure, touch, hot and cold.

STRUCTURE OF THE HUMAN EYE
Name _____

Label the parts of the human eye on the diagram below.

a. aqueous humor
b. cornea
c. pupil
d. lens
e. iris
f. ciliary body
g. vitreous humor
h. retina
i. optic nerve
j. choroid coat
k. sclera
l. suspensory ligament

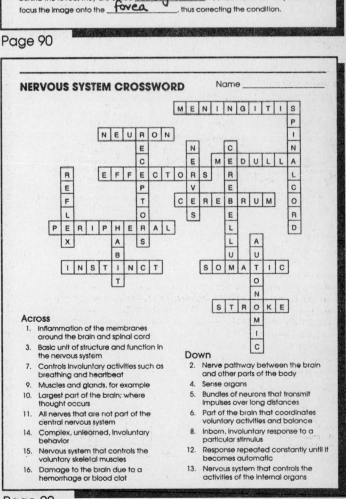

Fill in the blanks with the correct answers.

Light passes through a transparent layer, the _cornea_, which begins to focus the light onto the rear of the eye. Light then passes through the _lens_, the major focusing structure. The lens is held in place by suspending ligaments to _ciliary muscles_. Contraction of these muscles changes the shape of the lens and thus the _focal point_. The _iris_, located between the cornea and the lens, controls the amount of light entering the eye. The iris reduces the size of the transparent zone, or _pupil_, of the eye. The _retina_, in the back of the eye, contains about 3 million _cones_ which detect color and one billion _rods_ which detect light and dark. The central region of the retina where images are focused is called the _fovea_. The _optic nerve_ transmits visual impulses directly to the brain. People whose point of focus lies in front of the fovea are said to be _nearsighted_. If the point of focus lies behind the fovea, they are called _farsighted_. Corrective lenses may be used to focus the image onto the _fovea_, thus correcting the condition.

STRUCTURE OF THE HUMAN EAR
Name _____

Label the parts of the ear on the diagram below.

a. auditory canal
b. eardrum
c. hammer
d. anvil
e. semicircular canals
f. cochlea
g. auditory nerve
h. Eustachian tube
i. stirrup
j. earlobe
k. oval window

Fill in the blanks with the correct answers.

Sound waves beat against a large membrane of the outer ear called the eardrum or _tympanic membrane_. The _middle ear_. These vibrations are transferred by the three small bones, _hammer_, _anvil_ and _stirrup_, which increase the force of the vibration. The _stirrup_ presses against the _oval window_ which is smaller than the tympanic membrane. The _Eustachian tube_ connects the throat to the middle ear and serve to equalize air pressure. Hearing actually takes place on the other side of the oval window, in the _inner ear_. The fluid-filled chamber of the inner ear is called the _cochlea_. It accepts the wave motion that then travels through the vestibular and tympanic canals. Where the sound waves beat against the sides of the canals, _hair cells_ bend and _neurons_ transmit impulses. The _auditory nerve_ carries this information to the brain where it is interpreted.

The upper part of the inner ear contains three _semicircular canals_. These are positioned at _right_ angles to each other and are filled with _fluid_. The semicircular canals help to maintain _balance_.

NERVOUS SYSTEM CROSSWORD
Name _____

Crossword answers:
MENINGITIS
NEURON
EFFECTORS
MEDULLA
CEREBRUM
PERIPHERAL
INSTINCT
SOMATIC
STROKE
(down answers include: RECEPTOR, NERVE, REFLEX, CENTRAL, AUTONOMIC, PINAL CORD / SPINAL CORD, etc.)

Across
1. Inflammation of the membranes around the brain and spinal cord
3. Basic unit of structure and function in the nervous system
7. Controls involuntary activities such as breathing and heartbeat
9. Muscles and glands, for example
10. Largest part of the brain; where thought occurs
11. All nerves that are not part of the central nervous system
14. Complex, unlearned, involuntary behavior
15. Nervous system that controls the voluntary skeletal muscles
16. Damage to the brain due to a hemorrhage or blood clot

Down
2. Nerve pathway between the brain and other parts of the body
4. Sense organs
5. Bundles of neurons that transmit impulses over long distances
6. Part of the brain that coordinates voluntary activities and balance
8. Inborn, involuntary response to a particular stimulus
12. Response repeated constantly until it becomes automatic
13. Nervous system that controls the activities of the internal organs

ANSWER KEY

THE HUMAN ENDOCRINE SYSTEM

Name _____

Label the following parts on the diagram of the human endocrine system.

a. pineal
b. hypothalamus
c. pituitary
d. thyroid
e. parathyroids
f. thymus
g. adrenal
h. pancreas
i. ovary (female)
j. testis (male)

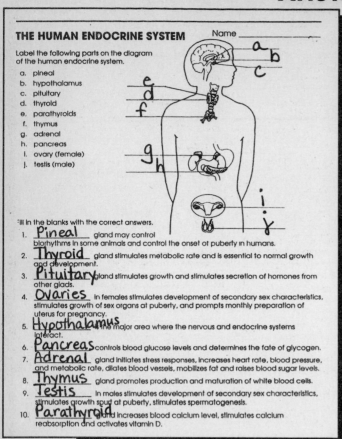

Fill in the blanks with the correct answers.

1. **Pineal** gland may control biorhythms in some animals and control the onset of puberty in humans.
2. **Thyroid** gland stimulates metabolic rate and is essential to normal growth and development.
3. **Pituitary** gland stimulates growth and stimulates secretion of hormones from other glads.
4. **Ovaries** In females stimulates development of secondary sex characteristics, stimulates growth of sex organs at puberty, and prompts monthly preparation of uterus for pregnancy.
5. **Hypothalamus** the major area where the nervous and endocrine systems interact.
6. **Pancreas** controls blood glucose levels and determines the fate of glycogen.
7. **Adrenal** gland initiates stress responses, increases heart rate, blood pressure, and metabolic rate, dilates blood vessels, mobilizes fat and raises blood sugar level.
8. **Thymus** gland promotes production and maturation of white blood cells.
9. **Testis** In males stimulates development of secondary sex characteristics, stimulates growth spud at puberty, stimulates spermatogenesis.
10. **Parathyroid** gland increases blood calcium level, stimulates calcium reabsorption and activates vitamin D.

Page 93

HUMAN HORMONES

Name _____

Listed below are the major hormones produced by the human body.

ACTH	epinephrine	insulin	prolactin
adrenaline	estrogen	Luteinizing hormone	progesterone
aldosterone	FSH	noradrenaline	testosterone
calcitonin	glucagon	oxytocin	thyroxin
cortisol	growth hormone	parathormone	TSH

Next to each gland listed below, write the name of the hormone or hormones it produces.

1. pituitary **ACTH, TSH, growth hormone, FSH, prolactin**
2. thyroid **thyroxin, calcitonin** **Luteinizing hormone**
3. parathyroid **parathormone**
4. adrenal **cortisol, aldosterone, adrenaline, noradrenaline**
5. pancreas (islets of Langerhans) **insulin, glucagon**
6. testis **testosterone**
7. ovary **estrogen, progesterone**

Next to each of the functions listed below, write the name of the hormone that produces this effect.

8. raises the blood sugar level and increases the heartbeat and breathing rates — **adrenaline**
9. causes glucose to be removed form he blood and stored — **insulin**
10. influences the development of female secondary sex characteristics — **estrogen**
11. promotes the conversion of glycogen to glucose — **glucagon**
12. controls the metabolism of calcium — **parathormone**
13. promotes the reabsorption of sodium and potassium ions by the kidney — **aldosterone**
14. influences the development of male secondary sex characteristics — **testosterone**
15. stimulates the elongation of the long bones of the body — **growth hormone**
16. stimulates the secretion of hormones by the cortex of the adrenal glands — **ACTH**
17. regulates the metabolism in the body — **thyroxin**
18. stimulates the development of eggs in the female's ovary — **FSH**
19. involved in the regulation of carbohydrate, protein and fat metabolism — **cortisol**
20. stimulates the production of thyroxin — **TSH**

Page 94

THE MALE REPRODUCTIVE SYSTEM

Name _____

Label the parts of the male reproductive system on the diagram below.

a. urinary bladder
b. prostate gland
c. urethra
d. penis
e. vas deferens
f. scrotum
g. testis
h. Cowper's gland
i. seminal vesicle
j. epididymis

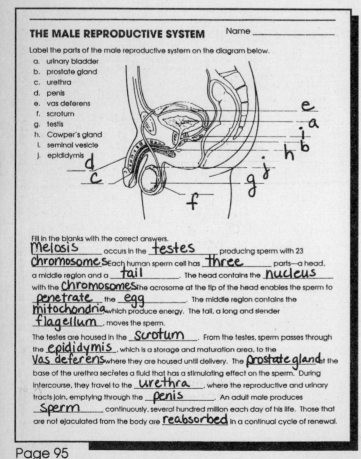

Fill in the blanks with the correct answers.

Meiosis occurs in the **testes** producing sperm with 23 **chromosomes.** Each human sperm cell has **three** parts—a head, a middle region and a **tail**. The head contains the **nucleus** with the **chromosomes.** The acrosome at the tip of the head enables the sperm to **penetrate** the **egg**. The middle region contains the **mitochondria** which produce energy. The tail, a long and slender **flagellum**, moves the sperm.

The testes are housed in the **scrotum**. From the testes, sperm passes through the **epididymis**, which is a storage and maturation area, to the **vas deferens** where they are housed until delivery. The **prostate gland** at the base of the urethra secretes a fluid that has a stimulating effect on the sperm. During intercourse, they travel to the **urethra**, where the reproductive and urinary tracts join, emptying through the **penis**. An adult male produces **sperm** continuously, several hundred million each day of his life. Those that are not ejaculated from the body are **reabsorbed** in a continual cycle of renewal.

Page 95

THE FEMALE REPRODUCTIVE SYSTEM

Name _____

Label the parts of the female reproductive system on the diagram.

a. ovary
b. uterus
c. urinary bladder
d. urethra
e. vagina
f. cervix
g. Fallopian tube

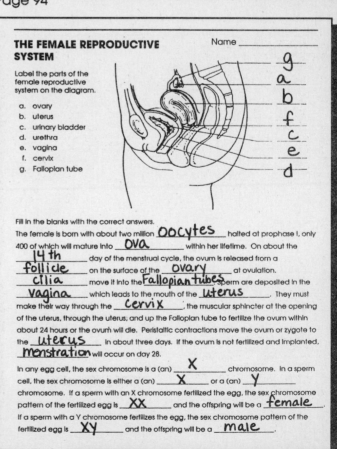

Fill in the blanks with the correct answers.

The female is born with about two million **oocytes** halted at prophase I, only 400 of which will mature into **ova** within her lifetime. On about the **14th** day of the menstrual cycle, the ovum is released from a **follicle** on the surface of the **ovary** at ovulation. **Cilia** move it into the **Fallopian tubes** sperm are deposited in the **vagina** which leads to the mouth of the **uterus**. They must make their way through the **cervix**, the muscular sphincter at the opening of the uterus, through the uterus, and up the Fallopian tube to fertilize the ovum within about 24 hours or the ovum will die. Peristaltic contractions move the ovum or zygote to the **uterus** in about three days. If the ovum is not fertilized and implanted, **menstration** will occur on day 28.

In any egg cell, the sex chromosome is a (an) **X** chromosome. In a sperm cell, the sex chromosome is either a (an) **X** or a (an) **Y** chromosome. If a sperm with an X chromosome fertilized the egg, the sex chromosome pattern of the fertilized egg is **XX** and the offspring will be a **female**. If a sperm with a Y chromosome fertilizes the egg, the sex chromosome pattern of the fertilized egg is **XY** and the offspring will be a **male**.

Page 96

A MAMMAL EMBRYO

Name _____

Label the parts of the embryo in utero in the diagram below. Give the function/purpose of each part.

a. embryo—developing offspring during the first two months of life

b. placenta—mass of tissue in uterine wall that exchanges substances between mother and embryo or fetus

c. Fallopian tube—tube from ovary to the uterus; here fertilization occurs

d. uterine wall—thickened, muscular portion of the uterus

e. umbilical cord—cord containing blood vessels that attaches embryo/fetus to the placenta

f. amnion—forms a protective sac around the embryo/fetus that fills with fluid

g. amniotic fluid—fluid that protects the embryo/fetus

h. vagina—canal through which fetus leaves the body

i. uterus—thick-walled organ in which the embryo/fetus develops

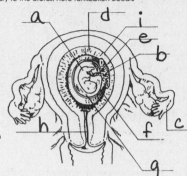

Fill in the blanks with the correct answers.

After two months of development, the embryo is called a (an) **fetus**. The **placenta** is formed in part from the inner lining of the uterus and in part from other membranes. It is through the placenta that the embryo/fetus is nourished while in the **uterus** and **wastes** are carried away. The **umbilical cord** connects the embryo/fetus with the placenta. It provides a transport system for placental-fetal circulation. The **amnion** is the innermost of the extra embryonic membranes, and it forms a fluid-filled **sac**, around the embryo/fetus.

HUMAN REPRODUCTION

Name _____

Fill in the blanks from the word list below. Words may be used more than once.

corpus luteum	implantation	ova	seminal fluid
estrogen	LH (luteinizing hormone)	progesterone	seminal vesicles
Fallopian tube		prostate	testes
follicles	menstruation	puberty	uterus
FSH (follicle stimulating hormone)	ovary	scrotum	vagina
	ovulation	semen	vas deferens

The production of sperm takes place in the **testes**. These paired glands are contained in a sac called the **scrotum**. The sperm travel to the urethra through a long tube called the **vas deferens** During this passage, **seminal fluid** secreted by the **prostate, seminal vesicles** and Cowper's glands are mixed with the sperm. This mixture is called **semen**. During sexual intercourse, **semen** is released through the urethra and deposited in the female's **vagina**.

The female gonad is called the **ovary**. A female is born with all the egg cells, or **ova**, that she will ever have, but they are immature. Beginning at **puberty**, the hormone **FSH** is released from the pituitary to stimulate maturation of a number of eggs. The eggs are contained in saclike structures called **follicles**. Usually, only one of the eggs matures fully each month. As the **follicles** enlarge, they secrete the hormone **estrogen**, which causes the lining of the **uterus** to thicken. After about 9 to 19 days, a surge of the hormone **LH** is released from the pituitary. This causes the fully developed **follicle** to rupture, releasing a mature egg. This is called **ovulation**. The follicle now becomes a yellow tissue called the **corpus luteum**. This body secretes the hormone **progesterone**, which further thickens the lining of the uterus in preparation for receiving and nourishing a fertilized egg. When the ovum is released during **ovulation**, it enters **Fallopian tube** and begins its journey to the uterus. If it encounters sperm during this journey, it may be fertilized and begin dividing. When the fertilized egg reaches the uterus, if all goes well, **implantation** will occur and a pregnancy will be established. If no fertilization occurs, the **corpus luteum** disintegrates after about 13-15 days and **menstration** occurs. Then the cycle begins again.

HUMAN ENDOCRINE AND REPRODUCTION CROSSWORD

Name _____

```
P I T U I T A R Y
A           H
N           Y       O   L U T E N I Z I N G
C           R       V       E
R       H Y P O T H A L M U S
E           H       R       T   T H Y O R X I N
A C T H     I       I       E           O
S           D       E       S           R       P
            P E N I S   T       V A G I N A       L
            R           H                 R       A
            O           Y                 E       C
            S C R O T U M   C       F     N       E
O V I D U C T       U T E R U S   A M N I O N     T
            A       S R   R                       A
            T       C R I               R
            E       V                   L
                    I                   I
                    X                   N
```

Across
1. Endocrine gland at base of brain
4. Hormone that causes follicle to mature
6. At the base of brain, gland that interacts with pituitary
7. Hormone produced by thyroid
9. Pituitary hormone that targets adrenal cortex
11. Organ through which sperm leaves the body
13. Tube leading from uterus to outside of body
14. Sac containing testes
17. Tube joining ovary to uterus
18. Houses developing embryo
19. Fluid-filled membrane surrounding embryo

Down
1. Gland that secretes insulin
2. Gland that secretes thyroxin
3. Organs that produce egg cells
5. Male reproductive glands
8. Hormone produced by adrenal medulla
10. Uterine membrane transports substances between mother and embryo
12. Ductless gland under breastbone
15. Neck of uterus
16. Hormone stimulates follicle production

TYPES OF DISEASES

Name _____

Diseases may be classified into several types; among these are inherited diseases, deficiency diseases, infectious diseases and hormonal disease. First, indicate the type of disease. Then, identify the specific cause of each deficiency, infectious and hormonal disease. For inherited disease, indicate whether it is sex-linked, the result of a defective gene or a chromosomal abnormality.

Disease	Type of Disease	Specific Cause
1. tetanus	infectious	bacteria
2. diabetes	hormonal	lack of insulin
3. hemophilia	inherited	sex-linked
4. common cold	infectious	virus
5. sickle-cell anemia	inherited	defective gene
6. measles	infectious	virus
7. Addison's disease	hormonal	lack of corticoids
8. anemia	deficiency	lack of iron
9. Down syndrome	inherited	chromosomal abnormality
10. AIDS	infectious	virus
11. night blindness	deficiency	lack of vitamin A
12. tuberculosis	infectious	bacteria
13. polio	infectious	virus
14. Kleinfelter syndrome	inherited	chromosomal abnormality
15. colorblindness	inherited	sex-linked
16. pellagra	deficiency	lack of niacin
17. goiter	hormonal	enlarged thyroid
18. diptheria	infectious	bacteria
19. rickets	deficiency	lack of vitamin D
20. pertussis	infectious	bacteria

ANSWER KEY

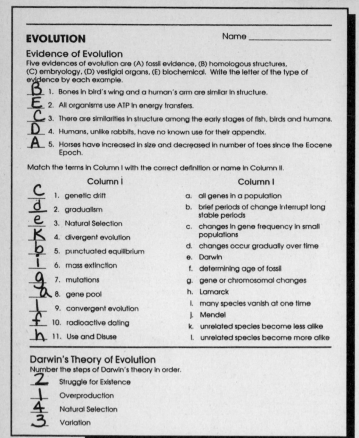

EVOLUTION

Name _____

Evidence of Evolution

Five evidences of evolution are (A) fossil evidence, (B) homologous structures, (C) embryology, (D) vestigial organs, (E) biochemical. Write the letter of the type of evidence by each example.

B 1. Bones in bird's wing and a human's arm are similar in structure.

E 2. All organisms use ATP in energy transfers.

C 3. There are similarities in structure among the early stages of fish, birds and humans.

D 4. Humans, unlike rabbits, have no known use for their appendix.

A 5. Horses have increased in size and decreased in number of toes since the Eocene Epoch.

Match the terms in Column I with the correct definition or name in Column II.

Column I		Column II	
C 1.	genetic drift	a.	all genes in a population
d 2.	gradualism	b.	brief periods of change interrupt long stable periods
e 3.	Natural Selection	c.	changes in gene frequency in small populations
K 4.	divergent evolution	d.	changes occur gradually over time
b 5.	punctuated equilibrium	e.	Darwin
i 6.	mass extinction	f.	determining age of fossil
g 7.	mutations	g.	gene or chromosomal changes
a 8.	gene pool	h.	Lamarck
l 9.	convergent evolution	i.	many species vanish at one time
f 10.	radioactive dating	j.	Mendel
h 11.	Use and Disuse	k.	unrelated species become less alike
		l.	unrelated species become more alike

Darwin's Theory of Evolution

Number the steps of Darwin's theory in order.

2 Struggle for Existence

1 Overproduction

4 Natural Selection

3 Variation

Page 101

ECOLOGICAL RELATIONSHIPS

Name _____

Food Webs

Use the food web below to answer questions 1-5.

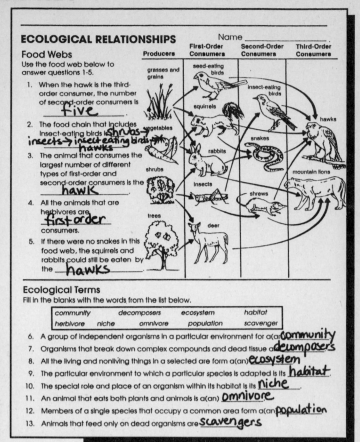

1. When the hawk is the third-order consumer, the number of second-order consumers is **five**.

2. The food chain that includes insect-eating birds is **shrubs→ insects → insect eating birds → hawks**

3. The animal that consumes the largest number of different types of first-order and second-order consumers is the **hawk**.

4. All the animals that are herbivores are **first order** consumers.

5. If there were no snakes in this food web, the squirrels and rabbits could still be eaten by the **hawks**.

Ecological Terms

Fill in the blanks with the words from the list below.

community	decomposers	ecosystem	habitat
herbivore	niche	omnivore	population	scavenger

6. A group of independent organisms in a particular environment for a(an **community**

7. Organisms that break down complex compounds and dead tissue a **decomposers**

8. All the living and nonliving things in a selected are form a(an) **ecosystem**

9. The particular environment to which a particular species is adapted is its **habitat**

10. The special role and place of an organism within its habitat is its **niche**.

11. An animal that eats both plants and animals is a(an) **omnivore**

12. Members of a single species that occupy a common area form a(an **population**

13. Animals that feed only on dead organisms are **scavengers**

Page 102